Infinite Place

Infinite Place

THE CERAMIC ART OF
WAYNE HIGBY

EDITED BY
Peter Held

ESSAYS BY
Carla Coch
Helen W. Drutt English
Tanya Harrod
Peter Held
Wayne Higby
Mary Drach McInnes
Henry M. Sayre
Ezra Shales

ARNOLDSCHE

To my children, Myles and Sarah,
and to my grandchildren, the three Os:
Olivia, Oscar, and Owen

© 2013 ARNOLDSCHE Art Publishers, Stuttgart,
Arizona State University Art Museum, Tempe,
Wayne Higby, Alfred Station, and the authors

AMUSEUM   ASU Art Museum
              ARIZONA STATE UNIVERSITY

EDITOR
Peter Held, Arizona State University Art Museum, Tempe

AUTHORS
Carla Coch
Helen W. Drutt English
Tanya Harrod
Peter Held
Wayne Higby
Mary Drach McInnes
Henry M. Sayre
Ezra Shales

ARNOLDSCHE PROJECT COORDINATION
Dirk Allgaier, Wiebke Ullmann

COPY EDITING
Wendy Brouwer, Stuttgart

GRAPHIC DESIGN
Karina Moschke, Stuttgart

OFFSET REPRODUCTIONS
Repromayer, Reutlingen

PRINTED BY
Leibfarth & Schwarz GmbH & Co. KG, Dettingen/Erms

PAPER
Galaxi Supermat, 170 gsm

Printed on PEFC certified paper. This certificate stands
throughout Europe for long-term sustainable forest
management in a multi-stakeholder process.

Bibliographic information published by the
Deutsche Nationalbibliothek
The Deutsche Nationalbibliothek lists this publication in
the Deutsche Nationalbibliografie; detailed bibliographic
data are available in the Internet at www.d-nb.de.

ISBN 978-3-89790-384-5

Made in Germany, 2013

COVER ILLUSTRATIONS
Dust jacket: *Pictorial Lake*, 1986 (cat. no. 24)
Hardcover: Preliminary drawing for *SkyWell Falls*, 2008
(cat. no. 51)

FRONTISPIECE
Wayne Higby, raku-firing, artist's studio, Alfred Station,
New York, 1998

PHOTO CREDITS
Carrie B. Bradburn: p. 85
John Carlano: pp. 24, 28, 33 (cat. nos. 12, 13), 50, 73
Nick Geankoplis: p. 150 f.
Susan Goetschius: frontispiece
Mahlon Huston: pp. 94, 178 f., 198 f.
Ye Jiangong: pp. 130 f.
David Morabito: p. 197
Steve Myers: pp. 45, 52, 71, 78 f., 186 (fig. 15), 188,
illustration on dust jacket
Brian Oglesbee: pp. 12 ff., 22 f., 25 ff., 31 f., 33 (cat. no. 14),
34, 37, 41 f., 46–49, 51, 54–59, 63, 68 ff., 72, 83 f., 86 f.,
99–107, 111–117, 118 f. (B. O.; Smithsonian American Art
Museum), 143 f., 149, 159, 161, 165–171, 174, 192
Lee Somers: pp. 141, 146, 160
John White: pp. 86 f.
Gerry Williams: p. 191

Courtesy of the Arizona State University Art Museum,
Tempe, Craig Smith: p. 35
Courtesy of the David Owsley Museum of Art, Ball State
University, Muncie, IN: p. 29
Courtesy of the Ford and University Galleries, Eastern
Michigan University, Ypsilanti, Robert Hensleigh: p. 21
Courtesy of the Minneapolis Institute of the Arts, MN: pp. 74 f.
Courtesy of the Smithsonian American Art Museum,
Washington, D.C., Mildred Baldwin: pp. 76 f.

Figures in Henry M. Sayre, "The Great Interior Basin:
Western Landscape as Container", pp. 59–67:
see credits in captions.

All other photos: Artist's archive (also hardcover illustration)

This publication has been made possible by the
generous support of:
Windgate Charitable Foundation; Marlin and Regina Miller;
The Robert C. Turner Chair endowment fund, Alfred
University; and the Friends of Contemporary Ceramics.

This publication is published on the occasion
of the exhibition:
INFINITE PLACE
THE CERAMIC ART OF WAYNE HIGBY

TOURING SCHEDULE
Arizona State University Art Museum, Tempe, Arizona
April 26 – July 20, 2013
Smithsonian American Art Museum, Renwick Gallery,
Washington, D.C.
October 4, 2013 – January 12, 2014
Reading Public Museum, Reading, Pennsylvania
February 8 – April 11, 2014
Philadelphia Art Alliance, Philadelphia, Pennsylvania
May 15 – August 3, 2014
Racine Art Museum, Racine, Wisconsin
September 21, 2014 – January 4, 2015
Memorial Art Museum, Rochester, New York
January 25 – May 29, 2015

Contents

6   The Man within Himself   HELEN W. DRUTT ENGLISH

8   Geographies of a Mind   PETER HELD

16   Acknowledgments   PETER HELD

Portfolio—Early Work

36   Ceramics, the Vessel, and the Paragone Debate   TANYA HARROD

Portfolio—Bowl as Vessel

58   The Great Interior Basin: Western Landscape as Container   HENRY M. SAYRE

Portfolio—Multiple Part Boxes

Portfolio—Bowl as Vessel

88   Ceramics as Ethos or Discourse? Wayne Higby's Contributions to Scholarship in American Ceramic Art
    EZRA SHALES

Portfolio—Tile Sculpture

120 An Auspicious Alignment: Wayne Higby and China   CARLA COCH

Portfolio—Architectural Work

142 Intangible Notch, SkyWell Falls, and EarthCloud: The Architectural Reliefs   MARY DRACH MCINNES

Portfolio—Architectural Work

172 Reflection   WAYNE HIGBY

176 Acknowledgments   WAYNE HIGBY

180 Chronology
200 Selected Resume
207 Selected Writings and Presentations
210 Selected Bibliography
214 Checklist of the Exhibition
216 Lenders to the Exhibition

The Man within Himself

HELEN W. DRUTT ENGLISH

What shapes the lives of others—their careers, travels, passions, associations to people, responses to art and nature? What makes a child of Colorado nurtured by a Western American landscape and horses, living a meditative existence in his mind, become, within himself, the man who loves China. For China was to become Wayne's Parnassus and Elysian Fields rolled into one.

As a young man in Colorado, riding his horse through the hills, Wayne Higby embarked on a solitary search. In 1963, the opportunity to travel presented itself, and his Grand Tour began—the lure of exposure to highly developed cultures and a journey indispensable to his education. Exposed to the Heraklion Museum Minoan pottery during his visit to Crete, Wayne's perception of art changed—as did his career mission from law to art.

In a flashback: My journey with Wayne began in 1973, when I encountered a unique landscape box in an exhibition entitled *East Coast Clay*, at Moore College of Art, in Philadelphia. Smitten, I wrote him a letter, inviting him to join my newly formed eponymous gallery in Philadelphia, which was committed to the resurgence of the craft movement. Upon the occasion of his first solo exhibition at the Helen Drutt Gallery, Wayne insisted on, and was responsible for, the wall of shelves being removed. This cast aside the assortment of his peers' pots—a grand decision that freed the gallery from a craft-shop mentality and forever changed my commitment in the eyes of the art world.

Countless exhibition opportunities have occurred since that time, ranging from nine solo exhibitions (1976–96) to group exhibitions. Interspersed with studio visits, we have explored his childhood through trips to the most significant sites of his life, as well as travels from Alfred, Reading, Colorado, and Philadelphia to Europe, Asia, and Scandinavia. We have indulged in intense personal dialogue, in seven a.m. telephone calls, that concerned the role of the gallery, family matters, the destruction of beauty, and shared concepts in response to career moves that included the selection of authors for essays. These conversations, as close to the ones that Kahnweiler and Picasso enjoyed, often can develop between an artist and his dealer friend. There were times I felt my brain was being pushed.

Among the roads traveled together we have been to Atlanta, Georgia, in 1983, at the National Council on Education for the Ceramic Arts (NCECA) conference, when Wayne was introduced to author Philip Rawson as we were plotting the republication of *Ceramics* (1990); when Wayne, artist Mark Burns, and I were on the road to Nara we reenacted the *Road to Zanzibar*, with Bing Crosby (Wayne), Dorothy Lamour (Helen), and Bob Hope (Mark). From Nara, Japan, we traveled to Reading, Pennsylvania, within one year. The hills of Reading leading to the Japanese temple brought the mileage distance closer, as we encountered Arrow International, Inc., the future home of Wayne's initial involvement with architectural installations.

Memorable moments included sitting in Marlin Miller's boardroom at Arrow International, discussing the forthcoming commission of *Intangible Notch* (1995), when it was suggested leaving the alcove and turning the wall so that the work could metaphorically join with the natural landscape seen through the large windows perpendicular to the wall. This allowed the exterior to be part of the interior. Can we forget the exhibition of *Landscape as Memory*, at the Museum of Art and Design, Finland, in 1991, continuing the ceramic dialogue between Helsinki and Alfred? Long walks along childhood paths in Colorado, before his exhibition was planned for the Colorado Springs Fine Arts Center, in 2001, made certain that I understood the influences of nature that informed the work. I also attempted to understand what formed this artist as we sat in the Alfred studio contemplating decisions about the porcelain slabs, influenced by Chinese abstract images on stone, and the decisions to remove the carved teak frame and hold the porcelain palettes with porcelain rocks.

Epistolary communication blurred the division between public and private from 1973 to 2002, when the letters ended, interrupted by the advancement of email, which coincided with the closing of the Helen Drutt Gallery. This was also a time when Higby's creation of large projects unified with architectural sites and enlisted private support from a patron rather than the support of public institutions and private collections for the acquisition of singular works of art.

Was it November 2005 that Dirk Allgaier and I journeyed to Alfred and the introduction to both Wayne Higby and Anne Currier was initiated? The seeds had been planted and the connection between publisher and artist was made. *EarthCloud* was published in 2007, by Arnoldsche; it documented the creation of the ceramic mural scape as it unified with the Kallmann McKinnel and Wood architecture of the Miller Performing Arts Building at Alfred.

There were many letters requesting meetings with Peter Held until that day, during the NCECA conference in 2010, when it actually occurred. Wayne was invited to join Peter at my home for lunch. The dining room, nearly dedicated to Higby's works, acted as a catalyst for further discussions between the curator and artist, resulting in this retrospective.

What is the role of a gallery director? Not to simply place works in public and private collections but to assist in molding a career and assuring that documentation of the artist's work will occur with dignity. I marveled at Wayne's transitions from sculptural forms as the large bowls thrown in Alfred were simplified. The movement from reality to abstraction coincided with "leaving" the object with the advent of major mural commissions.

Wayne first traveled to China in 1991. Things seen, heard, and smelled fused within him as he emotionally attached himself to that land. He responded to the notion that conceiving the earth as a living body and capturing that energy gives visual expression in Chinese paintings. The natural landscape is deemed sacred. Higby had begun to absorb those ideals as he created the *Lake Powell Memory* series, culminating in 1996—mystical investigations into the changing atmosphere of a special site for Wayne.

The concept of meditation and affiliation with Buddhist beliefs led to the erection of his teahouse, isolated from his studio and the main Alfred residence of Western Wayne; it sits on the edge of a secluded pond that itself emits an aura of serenity. A private place for a very private man who assumes an Asian sensibility as it moves slowly into his Western body.

Wayne joins other prominent writers, artists, politicians, and scientists whose initial journeys to China in the twentieth century changed their lives. Among them were economist-writer Harold Isaacs, Joseph Needham, David Gamble, Henry Luce, Pearl Buck, Thornton Wilder, and Richard Nixon. When you go to another place for the first time, do you establish an idea of what to see, where to go, what to study—what will occur within yourself? Phenomenological attractiveness toward China has produced another Higby, different from the one who roamed through the trails of an American mountain range. Wayne has poured into his work the soul and manners of a China that no longer exists, as he pursues the technical advances of a China newly discovered.

T. S. Eliot, in describing Henry Moore, asserts that art is, to him, the natural outcome of an activity in which the hands are as important as intelligence and intuition. He speculates about these artists who, through their achievements, become an exemplar to the next generation. Wayne is among them.

Geographies of a Mind

PETER HELD

It is a pity indeed to travel and not get this essential sense of landscape values.
You do not need a sixth sense for it. It is there if you just close your eyes
and breathe softly through your nose; you will hear the whispered message,
for all landscapes ask the same question in the same whisper. "I am watching you—
are you watching yourself in me?"
Lawrence Durrell, 1969[1]

Take a road that never ends
The rivers are long and piled high with rocks
The streams are wide and choked with grass
It's not the rain that makes the moss thick
And it's not the wind that makes the pines moan
Who can get past the tangles of the world
And sit with me in the clouds.
Han Shan (Cold Mountain), circa 750[2]

Wayne Higby is a consummately self-aware artist whose reflections on his own work are at once poetic, profound, and unassailable. The arc of his career tests one's grasp of how mind, space, and landscape coalesce. Early ascension placed him at the forefront of the American ceramics movement during an era of explosive growth and originality. It would be too simplistic to define him only as an innovator of raku-firing, although his iconic raku bowl forms made during the 1970s and 1980s are considered to be his signature works, his technique never gave primacy over content. As his story unfolds and as his breadth of work demonstrates, a broader perspective is needed for an artist equally committed to studio practice, and as well as his role as an educator, writer, and world traveler.

Defining Moments

Growing up in the foothills of Colorado Springs, Higby embraced the vast landscape of the American West. An only child, he found solace, joy, and mystery within the great outdoors with its craggy rock outcroppings, hidden caves, and majestic views of Pikes Peak. An acute observer with an intense curiosity, he found passion in youthful activities: horseback riding, high-school theater, and the arts. Classes taken at the Colorado Springs Fine Arts Center throughout his childhood provided an early outlet for his latent artistic talents. As he neared college, his father, a prominent local attorney involved in politics, tried to steer him toward a profession in law, but his son was doubtful this would be his chosen path. In 1961 he enrolled at the University of Colorado Boulder, where he concluded he was ill-suited to follow his father's vocation. Pursuing his interest in the arts, he became an art major with the idea of being a painter.

In his junior year he took six months to travel with family friends, visiting Japan, Southeast Asia, India, Greece, and southern Europe. For someone who had led a sheltered childhood, it became shockingly apparent in Calcutta, India, that humanity was far broader than first imagined. A self-imposed four-day quarantine in his hotel room questioned his role in the world. In hindsight, the experience propelled him toward a vision of humanity and art, which paved his commitment to teaching.

The group then traveled to Greece, which proved to be another epiphany that would encourage a lifetime in clay. Standing entranced in front of cases of Minoan pottery, Higby began to grasp the integration of painted motifs on three-dimensional forms. Ceramics never entered into his conversations with the art faculty prior to this experience, and when he returned, he sought out George Woodman, one of his professors who taught painting, drawing, and philosophy of art. Trying to assimilate and grasp the import of his enthusiasm for pottery, he was soon connected to George's wife, the potter Betty Woodman. No better guide was possible, and Higby focused on ceramics during his last year at university (fig. 1). Meanwhile a visiting artist at Boulder, Manuel Neri, imparted new perspectives on the burgeoning West Coast ceramic movement, revealing the work of Peter Voulkos, Henry Takemoto, and

1 Wayne Higby, studio, 1968, Omaha, Nebraska.

2 *Objects USA* exhibition, 1969. Wayne Higby's jar far right.

John Mason, among others. Higby was introduced to Paul Soldner, who came to the "Fire House" for a raku workshop (Betty Woodman taught ceramics for the City of Boulder Parks and Recreation Department; the facility was a defunct fire station).

Wanting to continue his studies in clay, the Woodmans, along with potters Jim and Nan McKinnell, urged Higby to consider studying with Soldner at Scripps College; Soldner was taking a sabbatical leave the following year, so an alternative was sought. Higby's second choice was the University of Michigan, where he studied with the iconoclast Fred Bauer, who was working on his slab-constructed sarcophagi series, and John Stephenson, a more calming presence in the studio. During his graduate studies, Higby focused on the evaluation and absorption of historical pottery: Minoan, Greek, Chinese, and Islamic ware held a strong fascination after his world travels. He continued his interest in raku-firing and experimented with Egyptian paste (a self-glazing, low-firing clay body) as a means to integrate surface and form. Visual beauty, a term many artists shun today, was embraced by Higby as he infused the past as he developed his individual artistic vision.

After completing his MFA, Higby was hired at the University of Nebraska in Omaha, where he taught from 1968 to 1970, followed by a three-year stint at the Rhode Island School of Design. This was an ideal time to be an emerging ceramicist, and Higby's work gained widespread recognition and acclaim. In 1969 he participated in the *Young Americans* exhibition held at the Museum of Contemporary Crafts (now the Museum of Arts and Design), New York, and in *Objects: USA*, and at the age of thirty, the Museum of Contemporary Crafts presented the solo exhibition *Wayne Higby/Ceramic Landscapes* (fig. 2). This meteoric trajectory not only provided validation and exposure for the artist but cemented his passion for teaching.

A Journey through Forms

Higby's boxes, bowls, and sculptures have been widely interpreted as three-dimensional landscapes in the tradition of American landscape art—an interpretation the artist patently and repeatedly refutes. Like the nineteenth-century luminist painters of the Hudson River School whom Higby greatly admires, the artist engages landscape as "the panoramic outer membrane of an inner manifestation of unity—a silent, unseen, unknowable resonance of coherence."[3] These opulent radiant landscapes evoked nostalgic, or elegiac, emotive personal connections with the past, in contrast to a topographer's matter-of-fact objective recordings of the present.

In Higby's creative palette, space is not bounded by the vessel's walls but stretches without limit as far as the viewer's eye and imagination will allow. Just as a model-maker fits a ship into a bottle, Higby, with a spatial mastery uniquely his own, nestles buttes, canyons, rivers … an entire cosmos in a bowl. Peering over the rim, the result is at once immense and intimate, horizonless and sheltered.

His early works, *Inlaid Plates* (1967 and 1968) and *Inlaid Luster Jar* (1968), were inspired by his multi-continent odyssey. The artist's eye for pattern coupled with his already deft craftsmanship elevates these novice objects, which in their timelessness marry decorative motifs of the past with the burgeoning eclecticism of their era. Swirling spirals, found in numerous Megalithic world cultures, are evocative of the Minoan octopus motifs the artist first viewed at the Heraklion Museum on Crete, emphasizing the circularity of form, creating a unified and abstracted whole. Squat in profile with a pregnant midsection and bisected quadrants, *Inlaid Luster Jar* (cat. no. 01) successfully unifies form and surface, carrying the viewer's eye by the repetition of pattern and its monochromatic copper-green palette. Although Higby salt-fired the first of the plates (contemporary salt-firing was still in its infancy and experimental stage, and hardly any potter escaped its allure during this time period), raku was to be his preferred firing method and would remain so for the next two decades.

In 1969 Higby traveled throughout the American Southwest, the West Coast, and the plains of Montana, which would further alter the course of his art and, ultimately, his life. This shift can be seen in *Partly Cloudy* (1970), one of the artist's first sculptural boxes decorated with natural imagery—clouds, mountains, sea. In this piece Higby reclaims the landscapes of his youth and begins to develop, through an ingenious combination of reduction and oxidation, the palette—turquoise, sea green, mottled rust, stony gray, and creamy white—that would become one of the signatures of his body of work. An ongoing interest in architecture and organized structure informed the box series, a format to harness nature's expansiveness into a contained shape (cat. no. 10).

For Higby, innovation in art was never about creating new forms but rather forging new connections, and for the next two decades he would conjure, bend, and unfurl space within traditional pottery forms. In "boxes" such as *Calico Canyon Overlook* (1976) and *Orange Grass Marsh* (1976), the vessel walls grow bulbous, the edges soften, until the form appears almost as an inverted bowl. Higby had only to turn the bowl right-side up to attain the "infinite space"—in the artist's own words, "space beyond the physical"[4]—that would seal his legacy as a ceramics innovator. Both works have irregular cut bases, reinforcing the ruggedness of nature itself. Inherent in the firing process, the variegated coloration and crackled glazes coupled with smoky raw clay surfaces elevate the visual drama of each work. The lumpen cloud formations serve as handles floating in space, acting as organic counterpoints to the more formalist base forms.

Over a decade, his box series would become far more elaborate in both form and imagery. *Tower Lands Winter* (1988, cat. no. 30), a tour de force, is perhaps Higby's culminating achievement within this series. Five interlocking lidded boxes are conjoined at right angles and, with their sheer vertical rise, provide a true sense of the expansiveness of a high desert plateau, on the magnitude of the broad range of the American West. With both ends contoured and eroded into gentle slopes, they bracket the center landmass, anchoring the work. Here, the artist works his illusionistic bag of tricks with the white ground contrasting the iron-streaked sandstone cliffs, projecting and receding space, pulling the viewer's attention into an imaginary center. Unfolding like Chinese screen paintings, a topographical storyline bleeds from one container to the next. The meandering blue waters zigzag through canyon lands, unifying interlocking motifs and color fields.

1   Lawrence Durrell, *Spirit of Place: Letters and Essays on Travel*, ed. Alan G. Thomas (New York: E. P. Dutton, 1969), p. 158.
2   Han Shan (Cold Mountain), *The Collected Poems of Cold Mountain*, trans. Bill Porter (Red Pine) (Port Townsend, Washington: Copper Canyon Press, 2000), p. 57.
3   Wayne Higby, "Reflection", 2012, this publication, p. 173.
4   Mary Drach McInnes, interview with Wayne Higby, Smithsonian Archives of American Art, Nanette L. Laitman Documentation Project for Craft and Decorative Arts in America, April 12–14, 2004, p. 53.

Intimate and Immense Bowls

During the mid-1970s, soon after arriving at Alfred University, Higby started in earnest to work with the large bowl form that is both universal and classic. Deeply committed to pottery with all its historical references and human associations, which he has poetically written about and spoken passionately on for decades, the concave and convex walls with their soft sweeping ovoid rims provide ample volume to mine his interplay of real and illusionary space. Freed from terra firma, the artist's works distill memory, feeling, observation, and perception into a unified vision.

Return to White Mesa (1978), with its thin flaring walls and eerily limitless imagery, attests to the magnitude and power of Higby's breakthrough. Its bone-chilling associations, conjuring stark winter vistas found on high desert plateaus, succinctly capture an austere beauty and remoteness. One can almost hear the wind wailing through sheer-walled canyons. His tentative investigations structuring space through blocks of color and his remarkable ability to convey a continuity between

3   *Study for Green Shore Landscape Bowl*, 1987. Colored pencil on paper. 18 × 23 inches. Collection of the artist.

inner and outer landforms belie not only the inventiveness of his work to come but also create a new vocabulary of the vessel itself. *Shelter Rocks Bay* (1980, cat. no. 19) is dominated by monolithic outcroppings of boulders, contrasted against a coral ground. The sweeping rim, accentuated by flowing waters, magnifies the inner volume of the bowl, providing the viewer with a freeze-frame in time and space.

He remarked during this period, "In my work, it is the commonplace bowl that serves as the known point of departure, the starting point for chains of associated memory. As an artist, I am in pursuit of a connection or series of connections between my emotional attraction to ceramics and my responsiveness to landscape."[5]

Throughout the 1980s and into the early 1990s, the humble bowl would grow into something iconic in Higby's hands—unbounded, mythical, shape-shifting. Just as Higby's "boxes" refused to remain boxes in a conventional sense, so the artist's bowls would begin to take on the contours of the landscapes they evoked. Higby served on the board of trustees at the Haystack Mountain School of Crafts for many years. Time spent on coastal Maine with its rocky shores and turbulent ocean was a dissimilar landscape from the Rocky Mountains of his youth (fig. 4). Beginning with pieces such as *Chimerical Bay* (1988, cat. no. 20) and becoming increasingly topographical and organic in later works such as *Midsummer's Bay*, *Emerald Tide Beach*, and *Storm Water Bay* (all 1991), a raw physicality not seen in previous works is evident. The light, too, becomes diffused, softer, making the clean hard edges of the past give way to more robust surfaces. Blue washes over a white ground capture the aqueous movement of the ocean or hint at a horizon dissolving into a shimmering haze.

5   Wayne Higby, "Innovation: A Matter of Connections," *The Studio Potter* 12, no. 2 (1984), pp. 20–22.

6   *Wayne Higby: Thresholds* (Buffalo, New York: Burchfield Penney Art Center, 2003), p. 5.

7   Mary Drach McInnes, interview with Wayne Higby, Smithsonian Archives of American Art, Nanette L. Laitman Documentation Project for Craft and Decorative Arts in America, April 12–14, 2004, p. 57.

Thresholds

To many observers, Higby's move away from traditional pottery forms and subsequent embrace of abstract sculpture may have seemed a break of monumental proportion from the rudiments that first made possible his spatial feats. To the artist himself, the cutting and moving of materials, beginning with the last of his sculptural bowls, led him quite naturally to the tile—the "building block" that continues to inform his work today. Inspired in part by his first corporate commission—*Intangible Notch* (1995, cat. no. 41) for Arrow International, based in Reading, Pennsylvania—Higby rethought his approach, working within a fixed architectural space on a scale unfamiliar with his past studio practice.

Lacuna Rock (1999), the earliest (and smallest) earthenware tile sculpture, introduces Higby's use of the threshold or gateway, a teasing opening through which light and intimation beckon the viewer to continue the journey. A freestanding slab of clay, *Lacuna Rock* conveys the loneliness of a twilight eve in this deserted landscape; an estuary snakes behind massive rock formations with its punctured opening, an empty space where imagination reigns.

Later earthenware sculptures, such as *Green River Gorge* (cat. no. 38) and *Eidolon Creek* (both dated 2002) place the gateway within a more textural and geologically traumatic agglomeration of outcroppings and ruptures. Higby still claimed to be striving during this period to establish "a zone of quiet coherence."[6] In the presence of these torn and enduring microcosms, the viewer may indeed feel that nature and human emotion have indivisibly fused. By extending that moment of passage, a slight delay, only for an instant, provides one that moment of insight.

Material Matters

In yet another seminal trip that would broaden his mindscape and prompt the series of porcelain tile sculptures titled *Lake Powell Memory*, the artist visited Jingdezhen, China in 1992. Higby had never worked in porcelain before and reflected, "What would I make? Well, the first thing you should do is forget everything you know about ceramics; just pretend you know nothing."[7] In the end, the artist took an approach at once iconoclastic and humble: he cut the clay into six- to eight-inch thick slabs and allowed the intense heat of the kiln-firing to crack and ravage the sculptures. To the surfaces of later iterations he added a *hua*—a subtle incised design inspired by a 1993 trip to Lake Powell, whose flooded canyon walls had left an indelible imprint—and then glazed the entire sculpture in classic celadon.

The result can be viewed in *Lake Powell Memory—Cliffs III* (1995), *Lake Powell Memory—Winter Rain* (1998), and *Lake Powell Memory—Recollection Falls* (1996), sculptures that belie their modest scale and seem to rise like massive rock faces shrouded in mist (cat. nos. 42, 48, 49). The strength of these

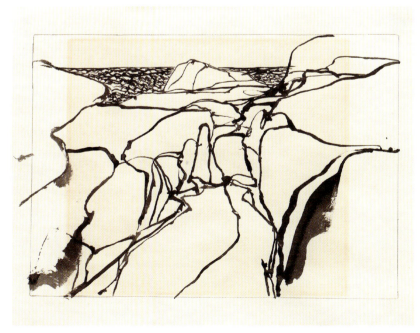

4   *Haystack*, 1990. Ink, brush on paper. 8¼ × 9½ inches. Collection of the artist.

sculptures' physical presence coupled with the delicacy of their surface imagery speaks to the power of Higby's submission to material and his embrace of opportune accident. Even in these closed, contemplative monoliths laden with historical references, Higby manages to create the illusion of infinite place in the melting, monochrome patterns-within-a-pattern in which East and West meld in sublime defiance. Imbued and fused with porcelain's rich history, these glaciated sculptures seem to be cleaved from a greater whole, remembered rather than observed

5   *Silence*, 2001. Rubbing, graphite on paper. 19 × 23½ inches. Collection of the artist.

directly. The last studio series before embarking on his monumental *EarthCloud* (2006/2012, cat. no. 53), *Lake Powell Memory* fully integrates the artist's aesthetic concerns: an alignment with earth and sky, matter and spirit.

Drawn to the Surface

Ceramics is a laborious practice, requiring a series of actions: design, fabrication, glazing, and firing. For sculptors, drawing is often thought of as a preparatory medium. The works on paper included in *Infinite Place* demonstrate another skill unbeknownst to those familiar with the artist's widely known ceramic work. A deft draftsman, drawing has always been an integral aspect of his art, helping the artist warm up and enter the creative zone. Earlier drawings, such as *Study for Green Shore Landscape Bowl* (1987, fig. 3), mirror the mastery of control related to the ceramics he was making at the time. Acting as blueprints, they become schematic studies, assisting the artist in visualizing his more complex forms and surface treatments seen in his bowl or multi-container canyon series. Given his virtuosic talent in creating illusional space, his drawings aided the transition from working through concepts to tangible objects.

His latter drawings—looser, more ephemeral and purely exploratory—"capture or conjure a feeling or mood."[8] As his work shifted from earthenware to porcelain and from color to monochrome, Higby's sculptures started to read more as drawings, where edges, volume, and weight disintegrate and become vaporous. *Canyon Lake 1* (1994, cat. no. 44) and *Silence* (2001, fig. 5) further articulate the subtle gestures and fleeting climatic moments he observed.

Expanding Space

In the mid-1980s Wayne Higby was first introduced to Marlin Miller, a 1954 Alfred University alumnus in the ceramic engineering program. Miller, a successful entrepreneur, businessman, and arts philanthropist, has been a steadfast supporter of the artist since their first encounter. Through their mutual friendship and admiration, a unique relationship developed heretofore a rarity in the ceramics field. Miller not only purchased individual works but also provided inspired opportunities that would alter and expand the course of Higby's studio practice. Miller's interest in the intersections of science, art, and technology stimulated discussions that eventually led to the commissioning of *Intangible Notch* (1995), *SkyWell Falls* (2009), and *EarthCloud.* Through the largesse and encouragement of Miller, Higby had to radically alter his approach, both conceptually and in execution. With greater expansion of scale, the artist worked with a diverse team of architects, studio assistants, and skilled tradesmen, finding solutions to highly complex architectural parameters and working with new materials and working methods. While the public works took the artist out of his former routine, he was able to continue his lifelong investigations of distilling the essence of land with all its visual potency. Linking the ceramic vessel, architecture and landscape come full circle, resulting in the synthesis of Higby's artistic vision.

Conclusion

If the landscape reveals one certainty, it is the exultant gesture that is the very genesis of creation endowed with humankind's record of activity. Much in the way that tectonic shifts and seismic waves move through the earth beneath its vast deposits of clay, continuously reshaping the landscape, Higby's travels around the globe have—sometimes subtly, sometimes dramatically—reshaped his ever-evolving body of work. Throughout his career, the artist has worked in a serial fashion: inlaid plates, covered jars, boxes, bowls, threshold-tiles, tile sculptures, and architectural installations. Each series informed the next engagement of forms and commissions.

Possessing the defining attributes of a formidable artist—exceptional talent and skill—a highly disciplined work ethic, and an unbridled enthusiasm for a world composed of subtle nuances and catastrophic events, Wayne Higby has consistently mined landscape as subject creating work that is unparalleled in the annals of the American craft movement. Through constant investigation and reinvention, he has extended the definition and potential of both the vessel and architectural site works in the ceramic arts.

6   Artist's studio, Alfred Station, New York, 2005.

Acknowledgments

It is always a great pleasure to have an opportunity to work with an artist who has made a lifelong commitment to his craft, who has excelled in all facets of his professional career, and whose work I have admired for many years. My deepest appreciation extends to Wayne Higby for his tireless efforts in making this exhibition and publication possible. He has been instrumental in my research efforts, providing necessary documentation at critical turns. On my visits to Alfred, New York, Wayne graciously opened his home, studio, and archives, allowing me to intrude in both his professional and personal life. My hope is that a wider audience will come to appreciate Wayne Higby's creativity and breadth of work over a career that spans five decades pursuing artistic excellence.

My gratitude also goes to Helen W. Drutt English, who initiated a conversation five years ago that brought Wayne's full range of contributions to my attention. She has been a steadfast supporter of Higby's career for many years as her foreword attests to. Without her assistance in fielding numerous queries and locating crucial works, this project would not have the curatorial rigor it possesses. Helen's life embodies the history of the craft field in the twentieth and twenty-first centuries; her depth of knowledge and palpable enthusiasm for ceramics and craft is unwavering.

The essayists for this publication are a stellar group of colleagues who deserve much credit for their reflective observations of Higby's life work. My thanks go to Carla Coch, who has traveled with the artist to China on numerous occasions; Dr. Tanya Harrod, a London-based design historian and craft scholar; Dr. Mary Drach McInnes, professor of art history at the School of Art and Design, Alfred University, New York; Dr. Henry Sayre, distinguished professor of art history at Oregon State University–Cascades Campus, Bend, Oregon; and Ezra Shales, associate professor at Massachusetts College of Art and Design. Linda White, from Alfred, New York, was invaluable in sifting through the artist's extensive archives and provided much needed organization for the compilation of materials utilized for this book. Individually and collectively, all have captured the essence of Higby's multifaceted career as artist, educator, and scholar. I owe my debt of gratitude to each one for their willingness to research and contribute to this publication.

Equally important to the presentation of the exhibition is this monograph. I'm greatly indebted to Dirk Allgaier and Wiebke Ullmann of ARNOLDSCHE Art Publishers, Stuttgart and New York, who have produced substantial art books worldwide. Generous collaborators, they have been sensitive in showcasing Wayne Higby's work to its best advantage. Also, I would like to acknowledge Karina Moschke, the graphic designer of this book, for her elegant design and making the publication reflective of the artist's intentions. Many thanks as well to all the skilled photographers, listed on p. 4. Through their incredible efforts, the artist's work has been interpreted to resonate in a different medium with sensitivity.

Infinite Place: The Ceramic Art of Wayne Higby will travel to five museums on its national tour after the inaugural exhibition opens at the Arizona State University Art Museum. I would like to acknowledge and graciously thank the museums and their staff for enthusiastically embracing the exhibition and attendant educational programs. The touring schedule, listed on p. 4, will provide an opportunity for a broad audience to become familiar with the full range of Higby's artistic output.

The Windgate Charitable Foundation has been a true beacon of light by supporting American craft and awarding their Artist's Exhibition Series grant for this project, providing the necessary funds to fully realize the exhibition and monograph, adding a new level of scholarship in the field. My heartfelt gratitude goes to the foundation's trustees for their enthusiasm and confidence in the project. A debt of gratitude is also due to Marlin and Regina Miller, longtime supporters of the artist, without the commitment of whom this catalogue would not be realized. Alfred University, too, was also a great institutional supporter of Wayne Higby's retrospective. My thanks go as well to the Friends of Contemporary Ceramics and its founding chair Linda Schlenger, for additional publication support and ongoing encouragement of the ceramic arts.

Many private collectors and institutions have been generous in loaning works for the exhibition. It has been a pleasure becoming acquainted with many who share as equal a passion for the artist's work. It is difficult to loan beloved objects for over two years, and I extend my heartfelt thanks to all of you. A complete list of lenders can be found on p. 216.

This exhibition and attendant publication would not have been possible without the institutional support of Arizona State University. My sincere indebtedness to Arizona State University president Michael Crow; Dr. Kwang-Wu Kim, dean of the Herberger Institute for Design and the Arts; Gordon Knox, director of the ASU Art Museum; and its senior curator and associate director, Heather Sealy Lineberry. Mary-Beth Buesgen, the Ceramics Research Center's program coordinator; Elizabeth Kozlowski, Windgate curatorial fellow; and Judith Amiel-Bendheim, community volunteer, were most helpful in research activities as well as handling the requests for rights and reproduction. To my friend the writer Germaine Shames, thank you for your inspiring writing and editorial skills. Anne Sullivan, registrar, and Elisa Benavidez Hayes, assistant registrar, managed the myriad of details with loan forms, packing, and transportation of works. Stephen Johnson, head preparator and his able design and installation team, always put the artist's work in its best light. It is my good fortune to be surrounded by such talented associates.

Lastly, I would like to acknowledge the support of all my friends, artists, and colleagues with whom I have been fortunate to work throughout my museum career. Too numerous to mention, they have enriched my life beyond expectation.

02   INLAID PLATE, 1967. Stoneware, salt-fired. 18¼ × 18¼ × 2 inches. Collection of the artist
03   INLAID PLATE, 1968. Glazed earthenware, raku-fired. 13½ × 13½ × 3 inches. Collection of the artist
04   BLUE CHANNEL, 1972. Glazed earthenware, raku-fired. 17 × 17 × 2½ inches. Collection: Austin M. Higby

RED WALL CANYON, 1975. Glazed earthenware, raku-fired. 17 × 17 × 2½ inches. Collection: Marlin and Regina Miller
CAROLINA WINTER, 1972. Glazed earthenware, raku-fired. 15½ × 17 × 2 inches. Private collection

WHITE MESA, 1975. Glazed earthenware, raku-fired. 13 × 13 × 11 inches. Collection: Sarah H. Morabito

08   GREEN TERRACE CANYON, 1975. Glazed earthenware, raku-fired. 13 × 13 × 11 inches. Collection: Marlin and Regina Miller
09   DEEP COVE, 1972. Glazed earthenware, raku-fired. 13 × 13 × 11 inches. Collection: David Owsley Museum of Art, Ball State University, Muncie, Indiana

PARTLY CLOUDY, 1970. Glazed earthenware, raku-fired. 14 × 13½ × 5½ inches. Collection of the artist

11   TRIANGLE SPRINGS, 1972. Glazed earthenware, raku-fired. 7 × 10 × 10 inches. Collection of the artist
12   CALICO CANYON OVERLOOK, 1976. Glazed earthenware, raku-fired. 13 × 15 × 5 inches. Collection: Jack and Helen Bershad
13   PILLOW LAKE, 1976. Glazed earthenware, raku-fired. 10½ × 9 × 8½ inches. Collection: Helen W. Drutt English
14   ORANGE GRASS MARSH, 1976. Glazed earthenware, raku-fired. 9 × 9 × 8½ inches. Private collection

15   FLASH FLOOD FLATS, 1975. Glazed earthenware, raku-fired. 7¾ × 13¾ × 9½ inches. Collection: John and Andrea Gill
16   TIDEWATER GAP, 1976. Glazed earthenware, raku-fired. 15 × 13⅛ × 9⅝ inches. Collection: Arizona State University Art Museum, Tempe, Arizona

Ceramics, the Vessel, and the Paragone Debate

TANYA HARROD

This essay tracks some postwar North American critical strategies in ceramics. By the late 1950s logic dictated ambitious clay work be brought into mainstream visual culture. A language would be forged through comparison and contrast with painting and sculpture. From the late 1950s onward, as a vocabulary for ceramics struggled to emerge, the writing was as vivid and as hopeful as the objects it attempted to dissect. The late 1970s, however, saw a call to order that took the form of a re-engagement with the past and with a multiplicity of ceramic traditions. In a historicist turn that was characteristic of aspects of postmodernism, writers and practitioners set about mapping a specifically ceramic aesthetic that focused on the vessel form and its global history. The aim was to resolve the problematic materiality of ceramic—in particular, its messy capacity to be *anything*.

1   *Study for Black Sky Landscape Bowl*, 1987. Colored pencil on paper. 18 × 23 inches. Collection of the artist.

The first, comparative, approach of measuring art forms against each other had respectable historic antecedents. As was the case with postwar American ceramics, the so-called Paragone debates of sixteenth-century Italy were born of status wars, registering the uncertain standing of painting and sculpture by comparison with other intellectual and imaginative activities. Leonardo da Vinci, the Paragone's most famous exponent, argued for the superiority of painting over sculpture and for painting's equality with both poetry and music. The debate—which drew in many other Renaissance writers and artists—led to the creation of workable vocabularies with which to discuss different artistic genres.[1] For most of us, the Paragone debate belongs with Renaissance studies. But comparing and contrasting the strengths and qualities of different kinds of art remains a seductive exercise. More to the point, during and after the Second World War the Paragone was central to the trenchant writings of Clement Greenberg.

Greenberg set out to define and differentiate, arguing in 1940 that innovative painting declared itself by its flatness and its "two-dimensional atmosphere," while sculpture needed to radically reject representation in favor of construction devoid of historical associations.[2] Greenberg explained that "purity in art consists in the acceptance, willing acceptance, of the limitations of the medium of the specific art."[3] Greenberg held on to the idea that sculpture and painting should maintain specific and self-referential identities. In 1949 he was arguing that sculpture offered more possibilities than painting. Released from "mass and solidity," sculpture could "say all that painting can no longer say."[4]

By the 1950s his strictures on the autonomy of painting and sculpture were to harden into an unhelpful orthodoxy, and in any case the hybrid practice of artists like Jasper Johns and Robert Rauschenberg—what Greenberg called "medium-scrambling"[5]—had begun to undermine his mantra of "pure painting" and "pure sculpture." But, as a way of talking about an art form, the Paragone continued to have its uses, not least in generating a critical language. It was a way of getting at the essence of a genre and of mapping a shift in emphasis. For instance, the sculptor Donald Judd's essay "Specific Objects" of 1965 was essentially a Paragone discussion in which what he termed "three-dimensional work" was measured against the sculpture and painting of the previous decade.[6]

1   For the clearest account see Catherine King, Di Norman, and Erika Langmuir, "The Paragone," in *Art in Italy 1480–1580*, Units 11–12 (Milton Keynes: Open University Press, 1979).

2   See W. J. T. Mitchell, "Architecture as Sculpture as Drawing: Antony Gormley's Paragone," in *Antony Gormley: Blind Light* (London: Hayward Gallery, 2007); Clement Greenberg, "Towards a Newer Laocoon" (1940), in *Clement Greenberg: The Collected Essays and Criticism*, ed. John O'Brien, vol. 1 (Chicago/London: University of Chicago Press, 1986), pp. 35, 36.

3   Greenberg 1986 (see note 2), p. 36.

4   Clement Greenberg, "The New Sculpture" (1949), in *Clement Greenberg: The Collected Essays and Criticism*, ed. John O'Brien, vol. 2 (Chicago/London: University of Chicago Press, 1986), p. 318.

5   Clement Greenberg, "The Status of Clay" (1979), in *Ceramic Millennium: Critical Writings on Ceramic History, Theory, and Art*, ed. Garth Clark (Halifax, Nova Scotia: Nova Scotia College of Art and Design Press, 2006), p. 4.

6   Donald Judd, "Specific Objects," in *Modern Sculpture Reader*, eds. Jon Woods, David Hulks, and Alex Potts (Leeds: Henry Moore Institute, 2007), pp. 213–20.

How does all this relate to ceramics? Ceramics as an art form in the 1950s did not lack a critical vocabulary. Between the wars the British writers Roger Fry, Clive Bell, and Herbert Read, whose thinking preceded and inspired that of Greenberg, created a critical discourse in which studio or modern ceramics together with selected preindustrial and non-European ceramics were admired as "pure form." Studio ceramics were compared with abstract sculpture and to modern music. But it was a limited writerly landscape, and although developed in Bernard Leach's 1940 essay "Towards a Standard," the chosen exemplars remained archaic ones—medieval pitchers and Song bowls—while the artistic goal was more anti-industrial than avant-garde.[7] The best ceramic criticism after the Second World War came not from Great Britain (with, as we shall see, one exception) but out of North America.

The necessity for a new kind of criticism had emerged on the West Coast by 1956. But an interview with Peter Voulkos in *Craft Horizons* that year indicated that articulating advanced ceramic activity was not going to be easy. Voulkos began by giving the potter's wheel its due, sounding not so very different to Bernard Leach or William Staite Murray for whom a pot was "born not made" through intuition, long experience, or by means of a Zen freeing of the spirit. He went on to argue that ceramics was a potentially greater art form than painting or sculpture because of its very limitations as "something that will stand up and function." He was not referring to utilitarian function. But he also acknowledged the superiority of painting, suggesting that painters make the best potters. He admired everything about Picasso, praising his versatility, the quality that Clement Greenberg was to disparage the following year.[8] As six photographs of new work published with the article make clear, Voulkos made full use of clay's capacity to be thrown, slabbed, extruded, and assembled, offering a daring autonomous identity for a new ceramics. The interview was also illustrated with a sequence of photographs of the artist at work, throwing, slicing, and assembling for the camera in a self-conscious shadowing of Hans Namuth's famous 1951 images of Jackson Pollock at work.[9]

This hint at a relationship with painting was to be further explored five years later in Rose Slivka's much-cited 1961 article for *Craft Horizons* "The New Ceramic Presence." By then Voulkos's pupils at the Los Angeles County Art Institute (later Otis Art Institute), including Michael Frimkess, John Mason, Ken Price, Paul Soldner, and Henry Takemoto, were making their own way, and Voulkos had taken on new students at the University of California at Berkeley. In early 1960, Voulkos had shown his work in the *New Talent* series held at the Museum of Modern Art (MoMA) in New York. These small exhibitions, held in the MoMA members' penthouse, were designed to showcase artists of any age who had not yet been given a one-person show in the city. Voulkos sent six paintings executed in vinyl and lacquer mixed with sand, and six ceramic pieces including *Sitting Bull* (now in Santa Barbara Museum), *Servillanos* (now in San Francisco Museum of Modern Art), and *Little Big Horn* (now in Oakland Museum). Each was four to five feet high, constructed from roughly collaged and thrown elements in glazed stoneware. The MoMA curator Peter Selz described them as sculptures and as "organically evocative forms of fired clay." The myth sprang up that Voulkos was ignored in New York in 1960, outfaced by the larger exhibition *Sixteen Americans* in the main galleries that had opened a month and a half earlier.[10] Admittedly he only made one sale, of a painting. But Dore Ashton wrote a perceptive review in *The New York Times* that favored the ceramics, noting how Voulkos created a "proper sculptural tension" by contrasting "a rough incised plane, irregularly glazed, with a full curving wall that is glazed to smooth perfection." She was impressed by the "intricacy" and majesty of the work in which she saw "the dynamic rhythms of dance."[11]

Slivka, who did not name individuals in her 1961 article, may nonetheless have felt something needed to be defended. After opening with a Whitman-esque celebration of the restless freedoms of America's "ebullient, unprecedented environment," Slivka goes on to argue for painting and sculpture as a twin inspiration for a ceramics that could, in theory, outclass them both. Considering West Coast ceramic techniques, she makes a comparison with abstract expressionist facture in which paint is "dripped, poured, brushed, squeezed, thrown, pinched, scratched, scraped and modeled.… It is corollary that the potter today treats clay as if it were paint." But another discipline enters the argument, as the potter "creates a sculptural entity whose form he then obliterates with the painting." For Slivka, "modern ceramic expression ranges in variety from painted pottery to potted painting to potted sculpture to sculptured pottery." Slivka was arguing for radical newness through comparison. But the force of her ideas was weakened by this concept of interchangeability: there can be no Paragone debate without difference.[12]

Two years later, John Coplans, a British-born painter and a gifted writer and curator who helped found *Artforum* in 1962, wrote a short note on Voulkos and his pupils in *Art in America*.[13] He noted the regionalism of what he called "ceramic sculpture," seeing it as characteristic of the unorthodoxy of West Coast art. Coplans, a colleague of Voulkos's, may have considered investigating this work on its own terms. But he was being told a story that was predicated on "a direct attack on the longstanding ossified craft approach" and which culminated in a flight from clay itself. Clay as material, process, and artistic genre was at that date not enough for Voulkos or for his pupils James Melchert and Michael Frimkess. Coplans noted that John Mason had an attachment to clay but recorded that Kenneth Price, despite his mastery of glaze chemistry, was painting his work with car lacquers (just as Voulkos had been using epoxy paints since the late 1950s). Here was a "movement" disowning itself, turning mostly toward sculpture. This disconnect continued on into the 1970s when we find ceramicists describing themselves as landscape painters, as sculptors inclined towards painting, or as balanced between painting and sculpture.[14]

Coplans, certain that something remarkable had happened in Voulkos's circle in the late 1950s and early 1960s, returned to the fray in 1966 to curate the show *Abstract Expressionist Ceramics* at the University of California at Irvine. Much has been made of the inappropriateness of this title and of Coplans's assertion that West Coast ceramics were "the most ingenious regional adaptation of … Abstract Expressionism."[15] Coplans wanted to signal newness and energy among a group of artists who sought "to rediscover the essential characteristics of the medium."[16] Because that medium was clay, Coplans could not help but record its problematic status in the history of Western art, even resorting to quoting Herbert Read's famous interwar pronouncement on the abstract nature of pottery. Coplans ended by identifying the development of Voulkos and his associates as a move into polychrome sculpture. If the message was again one of a departure from ceramics, the years between 1956 and 1958 were characterized as a peak—"the first radical movement to totally revolutionize the whole approach to ceramics."[17]

But if these radicals were turning away from clay, where did ceramics belong in the spectrum of the visual arts? By 1967 Peter Selz, Voulkos's MoMA curator, had relocated to the West Coast, where he curated the iconic show *Funk* at the Art Museum at the University of California at Irvine. This was a mixed-media chronicling of a San Francisco Bay movement that was "loud, unashamed, and free" with roots in Dada and Duchamp, and which combined highly personal painting and sculpture rooted

7   See Bernard Leach, *A Potter's Book* (London: Faber & Faber, 1940), pp. 1–27; on Bell, Fry, and Read see Tanya Harrod, *The Crafts in Britain in the 20th Century* (London/New Haven: Yale University Press, 1999), pp. 31, 34, 119.

8   Clement Greenberg, "Picasso at Seventy-Five," in *Art and Culture* (London: Thames & Hudson, 1973), pp. 59–69.

9   Conrad Brown, "Peter Voulkos," *Craft Horizons* (September–October 1956), pp. 12–18.

10   *Sixteen Americans* ran from December 16, 1959 to February 14, 1950 and showed Jay DeFeo, Wally Hedrick, James Jarvaise, Jasper Johns, Ellsworth Kelly, Alfred Leslie, Landès Lewitin, Richard Lytle, Robert Mallary, Louise Nevelson, Robert Rauschenberg, Julius Schmidt, Richard Stankiewicz, Frank Stella, Albert Urban, and Jack Youngerman.

11   Dore Ashton, "'New Talent Display at Museum.' Peter Voulkos Work Shown at Modern," *The New York Times*, February 2, 1960; see also press release for the *New Talent XIII* exhibition, February 11, 1960, Museum of Modern Art (MoMA) online archive; *Sculpture and Painting by Peter Voulkos: New Talent in the Penthouse*, February 1–March 13 1960, Museum of Modern Art, MoMA Archives CUR 658; Peter Selz to Peter Voulkos, March 18, 1960, MoMA Archives CUR 658.

12   Rose Slivka, "The New Ceramic Presence," *Craft Horizons* (July–August, 1961), reprinted in *The Craft Reader*, ed. Glenn Adamson (Oxford: Berg, 2010), pp. 525–533.

13   John Coplans, "Out of Clay," *Art in America* 6 (1963), pp. 40–43.

14   See *Northern California Clay Routes: Sculpture Now 44*, San Francisco Museum of Art, 1979.

15   John Coplans, *Abstract Expressionist Ceramics* (Irvine: Art Gallery, University of California, 1966), reprinted in *Provocations: Writings by John Coplans*, ed. Stuart Morgan (London: London Projects, 1996), p. 43.

16   Ibid., p. 46.

17   Ibid., p. 47.

in popular culture, using materials as diverse as fiberglass, plastics, metal piping, fabric, wood—and clay. Voulkos, now working mostly in bronze, was commended for his "highly funky endeavor to make useless pots."[18] As well as including pupils and associates such as James Melchert and Kenneth Price and the remarkable clay structures of the sculptor Manuel Neri, *Funk* also showcased figures like Robert Arneson and David Gilhooly who, while influenced by Voulkos, had taken clay in a figurative direction characterized by ironic wit that shaded into heavy-handed scatological humor. In fact their work could not have been more remote from the melancholy beauties of Voulkos's constructed monolithic forms.

In any case, the activities on the West Coast were only part of the story of ceramics at the end of the 1960s. One overview was provided in 1969 by Lee Nordness's *Objects: USA*, a traveling show of 300 items in all craft media, funded and ultimately acquired in its entirely by the S. C. Johnson Company (makers of Johnson Wax and a significant patron of art and architecture). The ceramics chosen revealed a crowded field. They included work by individuals whose careers were underway and respected before the Voulkos "revolution"—F. Carleton Ball, Maija Grotell, Gertrud and Otto Natzler, Edwin and Mary Scheier, Marguerite Wildenhain, and Beatrice Wood. There were also potters who made pots for use, or made work with strong ties to function—Val Cushing, Ken Ferguson, and Karen Karnes. The Voulkos group and the figurative West Coast group inspired by him were well represented. Voulkos himself showed a work in bronze. Other exhibitors were clearly not interested in function but were notably at ease within the ceramic genre. One such artist was the youngest exhibitor in the show, Wayne Higby, aged twenty-seven. He had already traveled in the Far East and had had a moment of epiphany in the Heraklion Museum on Crete looking at large painted Minoan jars. He noted in his statement that he was "impressed and influenced by the past" which he used as "a catalogue of ideas" to create objects in clay that express "concern with beauty."[19]

For the rest of the decade West Coast ceramics continued to be the focus of attention among curators from the fine-art world. *Clay*, curated in 1974 by Richard Marshall at the Whitney Museum of American Art's downtown branch, reprised the Los Angeles and Berkeley story, arguing that the febrile social atmosphere of California made possible a "university-perpetuated clay movement."[20] Voulkos was represented by, *inter alia*, the piece *Red River* (1960), which stood like a monument to an expressive abstraction in three and two dimensions. The link with abstract expressionism suddenly did not seem so far fetched in a show otherwise dominated by whimsy, bizarre humor, erotics, and clay simulacra and summed up by the critic Peter Schjeldahl as "slangy and informal" and notable for "extravagant peculiarities and semi-private languages." He observed, semi-approvingly, of figures like Arneson and Gilhooly that "it couldn't have happened in New York, where the achievement of a high style, in whatever medium, is the ruling artistic imperative."[21]

What came was not recognition but, rather, reaction—largely from within the ceramics world. In 1979 Margie Hughto, potter and curator at Everson Museum of Art, and Garth Clark, the author of a study of the potter Michael Cardew and of an anthology of writing on ceramics, staged the major historical survey *A Century of Ceramics in the United States 1878–1978*. At the accompanying symposium Clark spoke of the problem of clay's standing in the art world, arguing that the achievements of "clay sculpture" were questionable. He concluded that "the cutting edge of ceramic art is and always will be the vessel, which is our primary mode of expression, where there is no ambiguity in the use of form and where in the words of Herbert Read 'we can function as the most abstract of all the artists.'"[22] Clark had persuaded the critic Clement Greenberg to speak at the symposium but he had few insights to offer, suggesting that ceramics

18   Peter Selz, *Funk* (Berkeley: University Art Museum, University of California, 1967), p. 6.

19   Lee Nordness, *Objects: USA* (New York: The Viking Press, 1970), p. 86.

20   Richard Marshall, *Clay* (New York: Whitney Museum of American Art, 1974), unpaginated.

21   Peter Schjeldahl, "The Playful Improvisation of West Coast Ceramic Art," *The New York Times*, June 9, 1974, quoted in Richard Marshall and Suzanne Foley, *Ceramic Sculpture: Six Artists* (New York: Whitney Museum of American Art, 1981), p. 34.

22   Barbara Tipton, "A Century of Ceramics in the United States," *Ceramics Monthly* (October 1979), p. 54.

23   Greenberg in Clark 2006 (see note 5), p. 9.

24   Philip Rawson, *Ceramics* (London: Oxford University Press, 1971), p. 8. For Rawson's talk at the 1981 conference see Philip Rawson, "Analogy and Metaphor in Ceramic Art," in Clark 2006 (see note 5), pp. 35–52.

25   Rawson 1971 (see note 24), pp. 187–88.

26   Ann Jarmusch, "From *Mesas* through Canyons to the Sea and Back," *American Craft* 41/2 (April/May 1981), p. 11.

would have to simply "wait backstage for a while."[23] But two years later in 1981, Clark brought in the British historian of Oriental art Philip Rawson to address a second ceramics symposium. Rawson was the author of *Ceramics*, a phenomenologically inspired global overview that made high claims for the humblest pot as something that "'contains' both the reality of materials and process, and the inner realities of man's sense of identity in relation to his own world of meaning. Ceramics may thus be an important element in the 'world order' created by a culture."[24]

Rawson provided a compelling ceramic sensibility and vocabulary which bypassed the opticality of most art criticism and which honored all the proximity senses, above all the sense of touch but also that of sound. Clark was inspired by Rawson to pursue the vessel project, as a curator, dealer, and writer on ceramics. Potters too drew strength from the rich associative world conjured up by Rawson. Wayne Higby came across Rawson's *Ceramics* while browsing in a bookshop in the early 1970s and found it transformative. It is easy to see why. Chapter headings like "Memory-Traces and Meaning" and "Modes of Space" read like texts for Higby's mature work.

Higby's lidded jars of the early 1970s were decorated with stylized inlaid patterns that gradually morphed into suggestions of landscape, with passages of bright sky painted on the upper section of the piece *Deep Cove* (1972, cat. no. 09). In the early 1970s Higby was also making stylized "landscape" plates and the boxes *Partly Cloudy* (1970, cat. no. 10) with a cartoonish pop art quality, using inlay to delineate perky clouds, fields, and water. But within a year or so Higby abandoned this graphic approach that recalled pop artists like Roy Lichtenstein and Tom Wesselmann. Instead he presented garnitures of lidded boxes that explored the tradition of the American landscape sublime. Higby acknowledges the influence of the nineteenth-century painters known as the luminists. A comparison can also be made with the clear-air emptiness of the 1930s New Mexico landscapes of Georgia O'Keefe. Pieces like Higby's *Yellow Rock Falls* (1975, cat. no. 27), operate in two dimensions (employing painterly glazes) and, more literally, in three dimensions, with the groups of boxes projecting and receding spatially like miniaturized rock faces.

The effect of a hallucinogenic diorama was given greater force when Higby, in about 1975, began throwing and altering large bowls (fig. 2). In form they recall Lucie Rie's asymmetrical salad bowls, but for Higby actual functionality was not to be an option. The bowls also owed as much to personal memory as to the American landscape tradition. As a boy Higby enjoyed solitude, riding the trails of Colorado on a series of much-loved horses, taking in the unlikely colors generated by direct sunlight and deep shadow. The bowls also challenged the notion of decoration. They were employed by Higby to explore what Philip Rawson identified as "Pot Surface and Actual Space"[25] in *Return to White Mesa* (1978, cat. no. 23). As Higby explained playfully, "My bowls are for space. If you have a lot of space, you might fill it with a bowl."[26] In these majestic pieces, the reality of a painted landscape is offered in the form of two picture planes, one on the outside of the bowl and one on the inside. The collision created a startlingly theatrical vista with actual *and* perspectival depth.

Rawson may not have been directly responsible for these extraordinary bowls but his spatial understanding and his admiration for the pictorial logic of classical Chinese painting make him an ideal guide to Higby's aesthetic. Paradoxically, however,

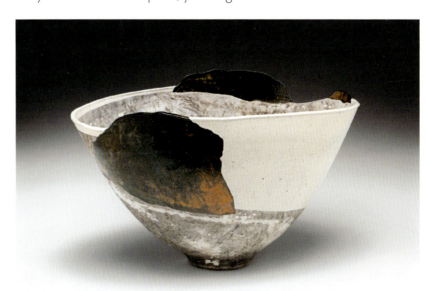

2   *Smoke Grass Basin*, 1978. Glazed earthenware, raku-fired. 12 × 21½ × 3½ inches. Collection: Sarah H. Morabito.

Rawson rarely referred directly to contemporary work, and when he did his conclusions were somber. How could meaningful ceramics be made in the shadow of "industrial-political-aesthetic complexes," in a world rendered two-dimensional by photographic images? How could modern potters develop the *richesse* of ceramic echoes discernible in Song bowls and vases or in hand-built Iron Age pots?[27]

By 1981 the "story" of American ceramics was being reconfigured. The new approach was set out in an elegant essay by one of Voulkos's most radical pupils, James Melchert. Commenting on the Joan Mannheimer Collection, Melchert paid tribute to functional pots, arguing that they too could be viewed as fine art. American ceramics were not about "inventing a new tradition," and Melchert re-presented Voulkos as an artist who had done more than anyone to reveal the historic nature of pottery. Melchert proposed a ceramic aesthetic that was indebted to Rawson's thinking, in which a key trope was the tension between the inside and outside of a vessel—as explored by figures like William Daley, Richard DeVore, Ruth Duckworth and Wayne Higby. Invoking the Paragone, Melchert saw the vertical axis of a wheel-thrown pot as analogous to the picture plane in painting. Like perspective in painting, the resulting symmetry existed to be violated. Melchert also discussed "decoration," a hitherto taboo word in advanced ceramic circles, paying tribute to the traditional wisdom of the pueblo potter Maria Martinez and to the orientally inspired strategies of Bernard Leach's pupil Warren MacKenzie as well as to the figurine tradition and that of kitsch ceramic knickknacks.[28]

Was ceramics being diminished by being brought back into its own tradition? Clay without context had proved alarming and critically unworkable. For the writer John Perreault it was, in its raw state, "too much like some other materials, excrement in particular." Perreault went on to note that "clay may have had a noble past, but in contemporary life it is as debased as it is ubiquitous."[29] Works of fine art could be made of neon, of rubber, of felt, of steel, and of rubbish. But clay remained problematic and was best dealt with by stressing its noblest associations. The vessel in particular appeared to offer continuity and existential power, representing "the physical and psychic life of humanity." These words by Wayne Higby suggest that, as much as anything, his own career can best be understood in the context of this return to a ceramic continuum. Higby has written eloquently and extensively on the vessel, reveling in the paradox of work—by himself, by his former tutor Betty Woodman, by Voulkos, Ron Nagle, Richard DeVore and Bill Daley—in which "function is conceptually denied while simultaneously allowing the formal and metaphorical implications of the pot to be explored by way of traditional pottery form."[30]

To return to the starting point of this essay, currently it would be a difficult exercise to discuss ceramics in terms of the Paragone. Advanced visual culture has more to do with relational aesthetics and sociological documentation while painting and sculpture are no longer central disciplines. Ceramics, meanwhile, can never reasonably escape its materiality. But that does not prevent work of great power being made in ceramics. And the vessel has turned out, of course, not to be the whole story. Clay is protean.

3 *EarthCloud*, 2006/2012. Glazed porcelain. 5,000 square feet. Permanent installation: Miller Performing Arts Complex. Alfred University, Alfred, New York.

The career of Wayne Higby, which this book celebrates, makes the point neatly. As we have seen, no one has explored and written about the vessel form with more eloquence. But Higby's work has gradually moved towards large-scale architecturally based installations—even if one of the most beautiful, *EarthCloud* (2006/2012, cat. no. 53), has continuity with the exploration of landscape in his earlier work (fig. 3). Again, Higby's turn to porcelain is imbricated with history. And, paradoxically, the first pieces that Higby made in porcelain, based on the landscape of Lake Powell in Utah— *Lake Powell Memory—Cliffs III*—take us right back to the Paragone (cat. no. 42). They are low reliefs, taken off carved plaster molds, and look reminiscent of the evanescent quietude of Chinese paintings. They also recall those old debates about the difference between painting and sculpture. As Michelangelo put it, "The more painting approaches the effect of relief, the more it is esteemed." His corollary was "the more relief approaches the effect of painting, the less [it is admired]."[31] But in the case of Higby it is more a question of fusion than of comparison and competition. Does that seamlessness defang the debate all over again and render us wordless? Or is it, as Higby argues, "just a feeling of cosmic sigh—it is so tedious that we have to continue to make choices."[32]

27 Philip Rawson, "Echoes: An Introduction," paper presented at *Echoes: Historical References in Contemporary Ceramics* (1983) in Clark 2006 (see note 5), p. 217.

28 Jim Melchert, "Images and Reflections," in *Centering on Contemporary Clay: American Ceramics from the Joan Mannheimer Collection* (Iowa City: Museum of Art, University of Iowa, 1981), pp. 9–17.

29 John Perreault, "Fear of Clay," *Artforum* 20/8 (April 1982). This article was a nervous response to a well-researched exhibition that concentrated on West Coast ceramics—Richard Marshall and Suzanne Foley, *Ceramic Sculpture: Six Artists* (New York: Whitney Museum of American Art, 1981, catalogue to the exhibition). Its timing was unfortunate, coming just at the moment when "ceramic sculpture" was beginning to be deemed a non-category.

30 Wayne Higby, "The Vessel: Denying Function," *Ceramics Monthly* 34/10 (December 1986), p. 29. The ideas of Higby and other vessel advocates were matched by similar ideas in Britain, in particular Alison Britton's identification of a pot with a "double presence." See *The Maker's Eye* (London: Crafts Council, 1981), p. 16.

31 King, Norman, and Langmuir 1979 (see note 1), p. 102.

32 Mary Drach McInnes, interview with Wayne Higby, Smithsonian Archives of American Art, Nanette L. Laitman Documentation Project for Craft and Decorative Arts in America, April 12–14, 2004, p. 61.

BAY CLIFFS MESA, 1984. Glazed earthenware, raku-fired. 11 × 19 × 16 inches. Collection: Louis and Sandy Grotta

WHITE TERRACE GAP, 1984 (two views). Glazed earthenware, raku-fired. 11½ × 18 × 16½ inches. Private collection

19   SHELTER ROCKS BAY, 1980. Glazed earthenware, raku-fired. 12 × 19½ × 16½ inches. Collection: Robert Pfannebecker
20   CHIMERICAL BAY, 1988. Glazed earthenware, raku-fired. 11 × 18¼ × 15½ inches. Collection: Barry and Irene Fisher
21   MAMMOTH ROCK BEACH, 1984. Glazed earthenware, raku-fired. 10½ × 19 × 16 inches. Collection: The Schein-Joseph International Museum of Ceramic Art, New York State College of Ceramics at Alfred University

22   FLOATING ROCKS BEACH, 1980. Earthenware, raku-fired. 12 × 20 × 16½ inches. Collection: Marlin and Regina Miller

After Floating Rocks Beach,
a large landscape bowl
by Wayne Higby

The sky is round, curving
into the rim of the world,
the edge of things. It is
the gentle curve of your arm
holding up the edge
of this planet, wrapped
in a circle like a dancer,
or the way a mother loves a child
with her forearm and elbow,
the crook to nestle in.
This landscape comes
from another time, the rocks
were towed by boats
in the foggy night.
They float in front of us.
At first you think these stones
are from a renaissance painting,
that they were behind the annunciation
of the miraculous birth
and have floated here before our eyes.
Then you hear the wind,
a steady wind that catches
in the crevice of your ears
the perpetual sound we are adrift in
the sound before sound had a name.

STUART KESTENBAUM
Director, Haystack Mountain School of Crafts, Deer Isle, Maine

RETURN TO WHITE MESA, 1978 (two views). Glazed earthenware, raku-fired. 12 × 22 × 13½ inches. Private collection

The Great Interior Basin:
Western Landscape as Container

HENRY M. SAYRE

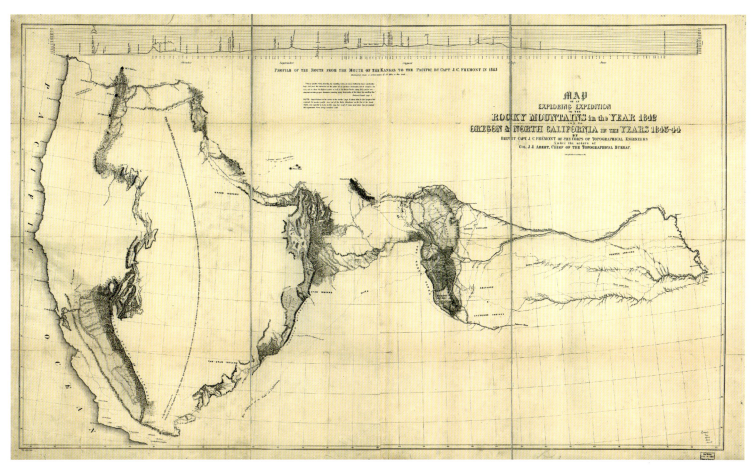

1 Map of an Exploring Expedition to the Rocky Mountains in the Year 1842 and to Oregon & North California in the Years 1843–44 by Brevet Capt. John C. Frémont of the Corps of Topographical Engineers under the orders of Col. J. J. Abert, Chief of the Topographical Bureau. Lithography by E. Weber & Co., Baltimore, Maryland. Courtesy of the Library of Congress, Geography and Map Division, G4051.s12 1844.f72.

On May 29, 1845, Bt. Capt. John C. Frémont of the U.S. Corps of Topographical Engineers set forth from "the little town of Kansas, on the Missouri frontier, near the junction of the Kansas river with the Missouri river" with an expeditionary force of thirty-nine men, which in just a few days short of a year later would complete "an immense circuit," circumnavigating what Frémont himself would call "the Great Interior Basin … a succession of lakes and rivers which have no outlet to the sea," and "which has the Wahsatch and Bear river mountains for its eastern, and the Sierra Nevada for its western rim; and the edge of which we had [first] entered … at the Great Salt Lake."[1] On a map drawn by Frémont's cartographer, Charles Preuss (fig. 1), a long curving line of text arcs across the blank white space that stretches from the Blue Mountains of Oregon in the north to the San Gabriel and San Bernardino mountains of California in the south. It reads:

THE GREAT BASIN: diameter 11° of latitude, 10° of longitude: elevation above the sea between 4 and 5000 feet: surrounded by lofty mountains: contents almost unknown, but believed to be filled with rivers and lakes which have no communication with the sea, deserts and oases which have never been explored, and savage tribes, which no traveller has seen or described.[2]

1   John C. Frémont, "The Expedition of 1843–44 to Oregon and California," in The Expeditions of John Charles Frémont, Volume 1: Travels from 1838 to 1844, eds. Donald Jackson and Mary Lee Spence (Urbana: University of Illinois Press, 1970), pp. 426, 592, 698, 700.
2   "Map of an Exploring Expedition to the Rocky Mountains in the Year 1842 and to Oregon & North California in the Years 1843–44 by Brevet Capt. J. C. Frémont of the Corps of Topographical Engineers …," in The Expeditions of John Charles Frémont: Map Portfolio, eds. Donald Jackson and Mary Lee Spence (Urbana: University of Illinois Press, 1970), Map 3.

2   Thomas Cole, *The Titan's Goblet*, 1833. Oil on canvas, 19⅜ × 16⅛ inches. The Metropolitan Museum of Art, New York. Gift of Samuel P. Avery Jr., 1904.04.29.2. Image source: Art Resource, New York.

Intentionally or not, the arc of Preuss's text serves to create a kind of three-dimensional space to his map, as if the text were itself the rim of a basin lying on its side across the western United States. And, intentionally or not, this great basin echoes in the actual landscape the other great basin of the day, Thomas Cole's *The Titan's Goblet* (fig. 2), one of the most mysterious paintings ever produced—in 1833—by America's first great landscape painter.

Like Preuss's basin, the scale of Cole's goblet is enormous. Perched on the far rim of the goblet are a Greek temple and a Roman villa. Boats sail across its surface. No steady flow of water spills from its rim; rather, it appears windblown, overflowing the rim in gusts. When the painting was first exhibited, at the National Academy of Design in 1834, the reviewer for the *American Monthly Magazine* could only comment: "We were, in truth, somewhat puzzled at the name of this picture, and confess ourselves to be much more puzzled, now that we have seen it … it is merely, and gratuitously, fantastical."[3] In 1886, the second owner of the painting, John M. Falconer of Brooklyn, New York, published a pamphlet claiming that "this drinking vessel of the Titans … is in fact, a subtle reproduction of the world-tree of Scandinavian mythology."[4] A tie to the Titans of Greek mythology is, of course, implicit in the title.

But despite all the theories seeking some symbolic meaning for the goblet, perhaps the most sensible is Ellwood C. Parry III's, who suggests that "it is possible that a basic visual analogy was at work in Cole's thoughts, an analogy between actual landscapes he had observed and the shape of the water vessels and basins he imagined."[5] Parry reminds us that in 1832, shortly before painting *The Titan's Goblet*, Cole had been traveling in Italy and had sketched the small, circular volcanic lakes of Nemi and Albano south of Rome, emphasizing "their circular form, the steep sides covered with trees and shrubs, and the absence of a natural outlet for the waters."[6] But these were by no means the only basin lakes with which Cole was acquainted. Even more familiar were the lakes near his home in Catskill, New York, where he took up residence in 1827, chief among them the North and South Lakes near one of the young country's first tourist destinations, Mountain House, on the Catskill Mountain plateau just to the west of Catskill itself. Cole often painted the place, as in his *View of the Two Lakes and Mountain House, Catskill Mountains, Morning* (fig. 3), all painted in 1844, the same year that Preuss was drawing his map of the Great Basin. I am not trying to suggest that Preuss knew of Cole's *Goblet*, but I do want to suggest that they were working from the same mind-set.[7] They were equally awestruck by the scale of the American landscape. Cole's lakes were drained by Kaaterskill Falls, but they lay in a basin not unlike the one he painted in the background of

The Titan's Goblet and the one described by Frémont upon first seeing the Great Basin from the escarpment above Summer Lake, Oregon, on December 16, 1843: "Broadly marked by the boundary of the mountain wall, and immediately below us, were the first waters of that Great Interior Basin." "In America," he meditates later in the text,

3   "Miscellaneous Notices of the Fine Arts, Literature, Science, the Drama, &c.," *American Monthly Magazine* 3 (May 1834), p. 210.

4   Quoted in Ellwood C. Parry III, "Thomas Cole's *The Titan's Goblet*: A Reinterpretation," *Metropolitan Museum Journal* 4 (1971), p. 126.

5   Ibid., p. 135.

6   Ibid.

7   It is, however, possible that Preuss knew of Cole's painting. Born George Karl Ludwig Preuss in Prussia in 1803, Preuss arrived in America in March 1834, just a month before *The Titan's Goblet* was first exhibited at the National Academy of Design, and he was employed as a mapmaker for the Coastal Survey, working out of New York (his 1837 maps of Long Island's north shore are available online at http://alabamamaps.ua.edu/historicalmaps/Coastal Survey Maps/new york - north side of long island.htm). The painting was exhibited a second time in 1838, when it was included in the Dunlap Memorial Exhibition at the Stuyvesant Institute in New York.

8   Frémont 1970 (see note 1), pp. 592, 703.

9   Clarence E. Dutton, "The Panorama from Point Sublime," in *Tertiary History of the Grand Cañon District*, with atlas. Vol. 2 of *Monographs of the U.S. Geological Survey* (Washington, D.C.: Government Printing Office, 1882), pp. 155–56.

"such things are new and strange, unknown and unsuspected, and discredited when related. But I flatter myself that what is discovered, though not enough to satisfy curiosity, is sufficient to excite it."[8] In fact, it might be that all Cole was attempting to suggest in his "fantastical" painting is this same excitement, his understanding that the American landscape is itself, like the goblet, the very work of the Gods—as vast, as awe-inspiring, as difficult to comprehend in its entirety as his imagined drinking cup. The goblet and the Great Basin might best be thought of as simple figures for the sublime.

The symbolic language of the sublime dominates American landscape imagery usually associated with altitude—with peaks, pinnacles, spires, buttes, promontories, and the views from such lofty vantage points, such as the panoramic vista of the Grand Canyon offered up from Point Sublime (so named by geologist Clarence E. Dutton in his 1882 *Tertiary History of the Grand Cañon District*, compiled for the U.S. Geological Survey).[9] But there is a second language, more domestic—and thus not so obviously sublime—but equally pervasive: the language of containers and vocabulary of ceramics. *Basin* is one of these words, and not just the Great Basin, but others across the American West, like the Columbia Basin and the Great Divide Basin in Wyoming. A somewhat small version of a basin is a *bowl* (the back bowls at Vail and the Sugar Bowl rock formation in Green River, Wyoming), and, of course, the edge of both a basin and bowl is a *rim* (the Mogollon Rim in northern Arizona and Rim Rock Drive in Colorado National Monument). There are more specialized kinds of containers like *cauldron* (the Devil's Cauldron in Oregon, and the related term, caldera) and *pot* (Teapot Dome, also in Green River, Wyoming, and the mud pots and paint pots of Yellowstone). And, finally, there is a certain vocabulary taken directly from ceramics: *slab* (Satan's Slab, one of the Flatirons above Boulder, Colorado, and, in ceramics, slab construction), *hollow* (as in both Sleepy Hollow and, in ceramics, hollowware), *plate* (as in the plate tectonics that inform the elasticity of the earth's crust), and, of course, *crater* (from the Greek *krater*, a mixing bowl).

3   Thomas Cole (American, 1801–1848). *A View of the Two Lakes and Mountain House, Catskill Mountains, Morning*, 1844. Oil on canvas, 35¹³⁄₁₆ × 53⅞ inches. Brooklyn Museum, Dick S. Ramsay Fund, 52.16.

VIEW OF PIKE'S PEAK,
40 miles distant from camp July 11th.
Lith. by E. Weber & Co. Baltimore

4   Charles Preuss, *View of Pikes Peak, 40 miles distant from camp July 11th*, 1843. By John Charles Frémont, *Report of the Exploring Expedition to the Rocky Mountains in the Year 1842 and to Oregon & North California in the Years 1843–44*. Sen. exec. Doc. 33, 30th Cong., 1st sess., U.S. Serial 507. Private Collection. Photo Credit: Gary Alvis.

Sublime is the word we have created to name the incomprehensible and the unknowable, the very condition of which leaves us, paradoxically, dumb-struck—literally, without words. The vocabulary of containment arises out of this muteness as a way for the imagination to contain what it knows exceeds it. This is precisely the gist of a story, written by Cole and included in his biography, written some five years after the painter's sudden death in 1848 by the magnificently named Louis Legrand Noble. "The Bewilderment," Cole called it, and in it Cole describes an excursion into the wilds of the Catskills. Wandering too far off the beaten path, he is caught in a torrential storm as darkness overtakes him. "No human eye could sound the black obscurity," he tells us, and suddenly, standing motionless, the ground gives way beneath his feet. "Deep water received me in its cold embrace," and he finds himself in a deep pool, "a dungeon lake," from it "water tumbling into the mouth of a cavern." Borne on the current, he plunges into the depths, giving himself up for lost, until suddenly he emerges into the open air:

> The tempest had passed over; the moon, now clipping the tugged outline of a distant peak, shot her soft light through the shattered clouds; a faint blush in the east announced the dawn; and the barking of a dog gave delightful intelligence of a house. Wet and weary, I once more picked my way through the vexing brushwood, and soon fell upon a path that conducted me to the log cabin, of which the dog had kindly given me the signal. A rousing fire and a venison steak came in pleasing succession, with many "wonder" and "guesses" by mine host, a rough but hospitable woodman. Among the most remarkable, was the wonder, how I came to get into the "pot," as he called the perilous gulf where I had spent a part of the night so delectably.[10]

10   Louis Legrand Noble, *The Life and Works of Thomas Cole* (New York: Sheldon, Blakeman, and Co., 1856), pp. 74–76, 78.

11   Frémont 1970 (see note 1), pp. 441–42.

12   Novak's writing on luminism is extensive. My summary here relies on her essay, "On Defining Luminism," in John Wilmerding, *American Light: The Luminist Movement 1850–1875* (Washington, D.C.: National Gallery of Art, 1980), pp. 23–29. The quotation on scale is from this essay, p. 28. Novak's commentary on the lateral edge and the panorama is from *American Painting in the Nineteenth Century* (New York: Praeger, 1969), p. 112.

That last word is remarkable, a word more suitable to a description of Cole's consumption of the venison steak than his harrowing experience. However, consciously or not, Cole has enjoyed, in the "pot," a taste of the wild.

Given his interest in landscape, it is no surprise that the subject of this exhibition and publication, ceramic artist Wayne Higby, today works in Alfred, New York, on the Allegheny Plateau just west of Cole's Catskills. But perhaps more important is the fact that Higby grew up in Colorado Springs in the shadow of Pike's Peak, a landscape that for generations of Americans has been the very embodiment of the sublime—it was, of course, from atop Pike's Peak that in 1893 Katherine Lee Bates wrote the lyrics to "America the Beautiful." Indeed, the first image of the peak ever seen by the American public was Charles Preuss's, published in Frémont's *Expedition* (fig. 4). On July 11, 1843, Frémont's party was camped "in that part of this region that forms the basin drained by the waters of the Kansas." Frémont goes on to note:

> The annexed [i.e., attached] view of Pike's peak from this camp, at the distance of some 40 miles, represents very correctly the manner in which this mountain barrier presents itself to travellers on the plains, which sweep almost directly to its bases; an immense and comparatively smooth and grassy prairie, in very strong contrast with the black masses of timber, and the glittering snow above them. This is the picture which has been left upon my mind; and I annex this sketch, to convey to you the same impression.[11]

Preuss's sketch is an early example of what would become a standard compositional device among nineteenth-century American landscape painters, especially among those who have come to be known as luminists, such as Fitz Hugh Lane, Martin Johnson Heade, Sanford Gifford, John F. Kensett, and Frederic Edwin Church. As defined by the great historian of American art Barbara Novak, luminist painting stresses horizontal formats in which planes take measured steps back into space, parallel to the picture surface. These "horizontal expanses … suggest, with their lack of accents at the lateral edges, that they are plucked from a more extensive panoramic view." The surface of the painting is smooth, almost crystalline (a feature realized in Preuss's drawing in the almost pure white surface of the snow-covered peak). And, perhaps above all, "the measured spaces of luminism are immense in scale, though small in size."[12]

Higby's jars and bowls could be described as three-dimensional manifestations of this luminist aesthetic. If they are not obviously horizontal in format, as we read their planar elements around their outside surfaces, the lateral edge of the surface seen from a single point of view extends with a panoramic sweep around the contour of the bowl. Looking down into a bowl, the 360° sweep of the landscape reveals itself—as if, in looking at Preuss's Pike's Peak, we could look down from above and see not only the mountains and plains before him but the expanse of the prairies encircling him from behind. The smooth, crystalline surface of the luminist surface is, if anything, even greater on the glazed ceramic surface. And—perhaps the defining characteristic of Higby's work—the scale of his objects is immense, the actual size proportionately small. Higby's vessels contain, paradoxically, limitless amplitude. In his boxes like the *Pictorial Lake* (fig. 5, cat. no. 24) and *Temple's Gate Pass* (cat. no. 29), the horizontality

5 Wayne Higby, *Pictorial Lake*, 1986. Glazed earthenware, raku-fired, 13 × 34 × 9 inches.

of his vision is more obvious, the five separate lidded containers in each piece grouped along a horizontal axis like a luminist painting, "as if plucked from a more extensive panoramic view." Each box is a form made of slab construction, and each stands beside the other in an intertwined geological convergence of sedimentary clays, a landscape of containers containing in its center, a "pictorial lake."

But it is Higby's sense of the sublime that most connects him to the American landscape tradition. While Cole can be credited with developing a general taste for the sublime in the American public, and while the luminists themselves always strove for sublime effects, creating what has been called a "contemplative sublime,"[13] the artists like Preuss who accompanied the Western expeditions of the 1850s, 1860s, and 1870s—especially Albert Bierstadt and Thomas Moran—soon raised the level of rhetoric to new heights. They fostered a new, "grand" style of landscape, and their aim was in fact to foster, in an eager American public, a sense of the grandeur and awe that they themselves experienced on their Western journeys. Writing about Moran, the great historian of the Western expeditions, William Goetzmann, puts it this way:

> He painted, quite literally, the sublime psychological reality of the West, in which if a mountain was larger than life, a cloud formation somewhat over-dramatic, and the rainbows seemed artificial, still it all added up to a portrayal of the impact of the magnificent scenery on those who were viewing it for the first time.... Moran's canvases called up in the viewer inner feelings of the sublimity of nature and the inconsequence of man. These were true emotions, recognized even by the roughest of Western veterans, who, critical of sham and unreality in portraits of the West, were among his greatest admirers.[14]

The same could be said of Bierstadt. He did not hesitate to exaggerate what he saw, but he managed, in overstating the landscape's magnificence, to capture its psychological reality.

The first of Bierstadt's canvases to draw the attention of the public was *The Rocky Mountains—Lander's Peak* (fig. 6). In April 1859, Bierstadt had joined Col. Frederick West Lander's survey of a proposed rail route through the Nebraska Territory to the South Pass of present-day Wyoming. By midsummer, the party had reached South Pass, just south of the Wind River Range and proceeded further westward toward the Wyoming Range. Bierstadt sketched along the way, and he tried, with not a lot of success, to photograph the scenery as well: "We have taken many stereoscopic views," he reported, "but not so many of the mountain scenery as I could wish, owing to various obstacles attached to the process, but still a goodly number."[15] While Lander continued on into the Wahsatch Mountains of Utah, Bierstadt turned around and headed home, apparently content with his collection of views.

Upon his return, Bierstadt took up space in the new Tenth Street Studio Building in New York City and set to work. *The Rocky Mountains—Lander's Peak* is the largest and most ambitious of the paintings he produced. By the time he finished it, Colonel Lander had died in the Civil War, and Bierstadt named the painting's central mountain after him. But the fact is, the painting bears no resemblance to the mountain named after Lander in western Wyoming, and in fact bears no resemblance to any place that Bierstadt had visited. It is an entirely imaginary scene, as invented a scene as Cole's "Bewilderment" is, too, in all likelihood a fiction. Indeed, Bierstadt has painted no American mountain, but a barely disguised version of the Matterhorn, the famous pinnacle near Zermatt, Switzerland, which he painted many times over the course of his career.

6 Albert Bierstadt, *The Rocky Mountains, Lander's Peak*, 1863. Oil on canvas, 73½ × 120¾ inches. The Metropolitan Museum of Art, New York. Rogers Fund, 1907.04.123. Image source: Art Resource, New York.

And yet the public took Bierstadt at his word. Writing in *The Galaxy*, in 1866, the essayist and art critic Henry T. Tuckerman marveled at its veracity:

> A few years ago the idea of a carefully studied, faithfully composed, and admirably executed landscape of Rocky Mountain scenery would have been deemed chimerical, involving, as it must, long and isolated journeys, and no ordinary risk and privation. And yet the American work of art which attracted the most attention, and afforded the greatest promise and pleasure in the spring of 1863, was such a picture. The accuracy of its details is certified by all who have visited the region; while the novelty and grandeur of the scene, and the fidelity and power with which the picture renders the magnificence of the mountains, their forms and structure, the character of the trees, and the sublime aerial perspective, have made this first elaborate representation of a vast and distant range—so long the traditional boundary of exploration and the haunt of savage tribes—one of the most essentially representative and noble illustrations of American landscape art.[16]

Tuckerman had seen the picture in April 1863 in New York City at the Metropolitan Sanitary Fair, a fund-raiser to provide health care and other services to the Union Army. It had hung across the gallery from an equally large work, *The Heart of the Andes* (fig. 7), by Frederic Church, Thomas Cole's student and heir apparent. The public had seen Church's painting before, first in 1859, when it had attracted 12,000 visitors in three weeks at its New York premier at Lyrique Hall. It was housed in an elaborate window-like frame, illuminated in a darkened room by concealed skylights, and surrounded

13 See Earl A. Powell, "Luminism and the American Sublime," in Wilmerding 1980 (see note 12), p. 80.

14 William H. Goetzmann, *Exploration and Empire: The Explorer and the Scientist in the Winning of the American West* (1966; repr., New York: History Book Club, 1993), pp. 503–04.

15 Quoted in Gordon Hendricks, *Albert Bierstadt: Painter of the American West* (New York: Abrams, 1974), p. 63.

16 H. T. Tuckerman, "Albert Bierstadt," *The Galaxy: An Illustrated Magazine of Entertaining Reading* 1 (May 1, 1866–August 15, 1866), pp. 679–80.

7   Frederic Church, *Heart of the Andes*, 1859. Oil on canvas, 66⅛ × 119¼ inches. The Metropolitan Museum of Art, New York. Bequest of Margaret E. Dows, 1909.09.95. Image source: Art Resource, New York.

by potted plants that Church had himself brought back from his expeditions to Ecuador and Columbia. Viewers were stunned by the painting. Without a hint of his usual cynicism, Mark Twain, who first saw the painting in 1861 after it was moved to the gallery of the Tenth Street Studio Building, called it "the most wonderfully beautiful painting this city has ever seen." "We took the opera glass," he wrote, "and examined its beauties minutely, for the naked eye cannot discern the little wayside flowers, and soft shadows and patches of sunshine, and half-hidden bunches of grass and jets of water which form some of its most enchanting features."[17]

But in the unstated but very real competition between the two paintings at the Metropolitan Sanitary Fair, Bierstadt's painting won hands down. His subject was, after all, what Tuckerman called, "eminently national.... [It represents] all that is most vast, characteristic, and beautiful in North American scenery."[18] That said, both paintings have much in common: close attention to the flora and fauna of their respective continents, and to the dress and costume of their peoples; a cascade falling into a lake that lies in a middle ground of almost pastoral serenity; mountain peaks surrounding the panoramic sweep of the composition; and, perhaps above all, a size of canvas commensurate with the scale of the scene, a fact that distinguishes their painting from the small size if grand scale of their luminist contemporaries. In fact, it is likely that Bierstadt, in taking a studio in the Tenth Street Studio Building where *Heart of the Andes* was on display, composed *The Rocky Mountains* with Church's painting in mind.

But it is worth emphasizing that the landscapes of these two seminal realizations of the sublime are composed around central basins. If for the artist-explorers of the nineteenth century "verticality was prized," as William H. Goetzmann put it, water rolls down from a rim of vertical peaks into bowls filled with mountain lakes. It is as if the viewer is gathered into and contained within the hands of a vast, unknowable God. Bierstadt returned to this basic compositional view time and time again, and in almost every case (with the possible exception of Yosemite, which not even Bierstadt could exaggerate) the view is totally imaginary, or rather, a freely realized representation not so much of any given place itself but of the feelings of awe it evoked in him.

17   Samuel L. Clemens to Orion Clemens, 18 March 1861, in *Mark Twain's Letters, Volume 1: 1853–1866*, eds. Edgar Marquess Branch, Michael B. Frank, Kenneth M. Sanderson, and Harriet Elinor Smith (Berkeley: University of California Press, 1988), p. 117.
18   Tuckerman 1866 (see note 16), p. 682.
19   Quoted in *Our Native Land: or, Glance at American Scenery and Places with Sketches of Life and Character*, ed. George T. Ferris (New York: D. Appleton and Co., 1889), p. 26.
20   Quoted in Donald Worster, *A River Running West: The Life of John Wesley Powell* (New York: Oxford University Press, 2001), p. 306.

It is as much depth as it is verticality that defines the American sublime. In the summer of 1873, Moran was traveling along the rim of the Grand Canyon with John Wesley Powell, who had first descended down the Colorado River through the canyon in 1869, when he witnessed a dramatic thunderstorm, described by Jack Colburn, a writer from New York who was accompanying the artist:

> Here we beheld one of the most awful scenes upon our globe.... A terrific thunderstorm burst over the cañon. The lightning flashed from crag to crag. A thousand streams gathered on the surrounding plains, and dashed down into the depths.... The vast chasm which we saw before us ... was nearly seven thousand feet deep.[19]

The scene recreates, in the Grand Canyon and some forty years later, the thunderstorm that Cole survived in "The Bewilderment." If Moran did not actually descend into the "pot," he did so imaginatively. When he returned to his studio in Newark, New Jersey, he recreated the moment in his *Chasm of the Colorado* (fig. 8). As the work was in progress, he wrote to Powell that he had "got our storm in good."[20] In July 1874, a joint committee of Congress voted to purchase the painting for $10,000 and hang it in the Senate lobby. In his large-scale installation work, Higby aspires to the same grand statements. *EarthCloud*, in the Miller Performing Arts Building at Alfred University, where Higby has taught since 1973, celebrates the Kanakadea Valley (in the Seneca Indian language *kanakadea* means "where earth meets sky") in a thirty-by-sixty-foot installation consisting of over 6,000 slabs of porcelain. *SkyWell Falls*, a forty-foot-high installation of some 352 tiles in the Performing Arts Center of Reading Area Community College, Reading, Pennsylvania, was inspired by Ian Baker's 2004 book *The Heart of the World: A Journey to the Last Secret Place*, the Tsangpo Gorge in the Himalayas where a legendary waterfall drops into what Higby has called "the deepest place on earth."

It is out of these two traditions—the luminist and the "grand" styles of American landscape painting—that Wayne Higby's ceramic work arises. It is not only possible to see the landscape as ceramics made large; the ceramic arts are also, after all, the closest of all arts to the land, fashioned out of the earth's very clays. But it is Higby's sense of the sublime that connects him most closely to this tradition, his sense that his work somehow contains the uncontainable, capturing—in his words—"the silent, unseen, unknowable resonance of coherence" that is the American sublime.

8 Thomas Moran, *The Chasm of the Colorado*, 1873–74. Oil on canvas mounted on aluminum, 84⅜ × 144¾ inches. Smithsonian American Art Museum, Washington, D.C., L. 1968.84.2. Lent by the U.S. Department of the Interior Museum.

PICTORIAL LAKE, 1986 (detail). Glazed earthenware, raku-fired. 13 × 34 × 9 inches. Collection: Sarah H. Morabito

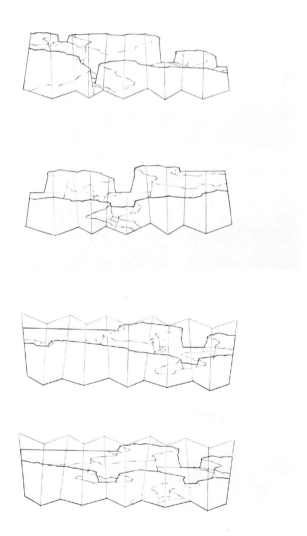

25 STUDY FOR CATHEDRAL GAP, 1988. Graphite pencil on paper. 12 × 15 inches. Collection of the artist
26 STUDY FOR EMERALD LAKE, 1988. Graphite pencil on paper. 12 × 15 inches. Collection of the artist
27 YELLOW ROCK FALLS, 1975. Glazed earthenware, raku-fired. 14 × 29 × 7½ inches. Collection: Robert Pfannebecker

28   PAINTED ROCKS CANYON, 1981 (two views). Glazed earthenware, raku-fired. 14 × 20½ × 19 inches. Collection: Minneapolis Institute of the Arts, Minnesota

TEMPLE'S GATE PASS, 1988. Glazed earthenware, raku-fired. 14½ × 34 × 6 inches. Collection: Smithsonian American Art Museum, Washington, D.C.

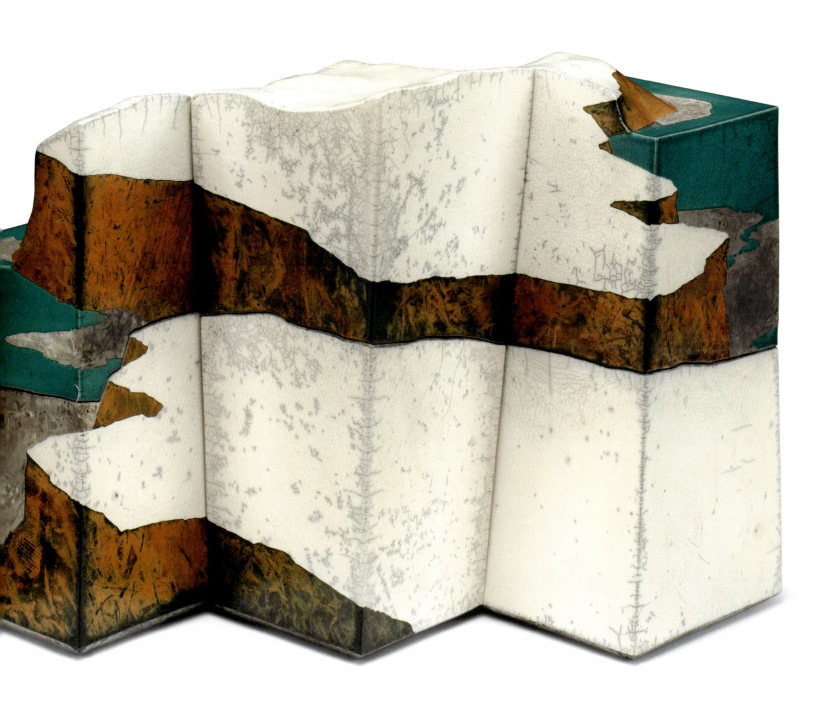

30   TOWER LANDS WINTER, 1988 (two views). Glazed earthenware, raku-fired. 15 × 35½ × 8½ inches. Collection: Arizona State University Art Museum, Tempe

31 MOON WATER BAY, 1990. Glazed earthenware. 12 × 12 × 16 inches. Collection: Marlin and Regina Miller

32 NIGHT SANDS REACH, 1991. Glazed earthenware, raku-fired. 11½ × 18¾ × 14¼ inches. Collection: John and Lenel Srochi Meyerhoff
33 EMERALD TIDE BEACH, 1991. Glazed earthenware, raku-fired. 12 × 20 × 15 inches. Collection: Linda Schlenger

34   STORM WATER BAY, 1991. Glazed earthenware, raku-fired. 12½ × 19¾ × 14 inches. Collection: Eugene Mercy
35   MIDSUMMER'S BAY, 1991. Glazed earthenware, raku-fired. 13 × 18½ × 17 inches. Collection: Sarah H. Morabito

Ceramics as Ethos or Discourse? Wayne Higby's Contributions to Scholarship in American Ceramic Art

EZRA SHALES

Wayne Higby's calm and gracious foreword to the 1984 edition of Philip Rawson's *Ceramics* (1971) is one of the stateliest greetings an artist has ever given to a work of art history. Higby appraised the work as a lasting contribution to art appreciation—apt, as the book still stands as an entry into what remains a field stashed in either the attic or basement of art history. Higby also offered a critique that was pleasantly free from the usual art talk driven by emotion, theoretical jargon, or autobiography. However, I did not share his view that critical writing on ceramics was absent from library or bookstore shelves. "Unfortunately," Higby wrote, "in the case of ceramic art criticism a void remains, principally because a thorough understanding of the details that define ceramics is not yet considered absolutely necessary as background for the critical analysis of ceramic art."[1] I stubbed my toe on this sentence because Higby's suggestion is that complex theory is absent—and that the corrective is both increased abstraction as well as attention to the specific molecular structure of clay. Had not Rawson delivered? He bypassed the issue of hierarchy and stated with complete certainty that a pot was a document of complex human thought and action that could, in the finest examples, articulate cultural ideals. What was wrong with specialized literature that focused on, for example, Meissen figures or Mimbres bowls? If good description was good criticism, there was plenty. It seemed that two paradigms, textual interpretation and staying closer to the earth, near to the medium's power, were at odds, or at least posed a paradoxical challenge for ceramicists.[2]

While teaching for four decades at Alfred University, an Olympian perch because it is one of the few places in the world where ceramics is a school's *raison d'être* and not merely a course of study, Higby has become a spokesman for the medium. His publications emphasize three commitments: the importance of the vessel as an art form, progressive educational ideals, and an unwavering faith in clay's power. His hours dedicated to academic conferences held under the auspices of such organizations as the National Council on Education for the Ceramic Arts (NCECA) and other craft-oriented organizations, to juried exhibitions, and to authoring articles for publication in conference proceedings and magazines such as *Ceramics Monthly*, *Studio Potter*, and *American Ceramics* have thus far eluded summary or evaluation. His art stands in the monumental collections and catalogues—but what of his words, such as this foreword? Do his students read these and critique them with their students? Does Higby's foreword itself reside in the category of criticism, of history, or is it merely an adjunct of his praxis? Were his views representative or influential, or both?[3]

Looking back at conference transcripts and periodicals from the 1980s one finds this peculiar declaration insistent—that clay suffers from an absence of theoretical and critical discourse. The cry is peculiar because the platforms were numerous and seemingly well-funded, and the criers included not only artists but also remarkably prolific writers, such as John Perreault, Garth Clark, Janet Koplos, and even Rawson himself. The indictment is still true today if measured by the exceedingly congratulatory nature of most exhibition reviews which make little effort to establish objective criteria. In retrospect, 1980s' criticism was more optimistic and pluralistic than today's. At the time, it was not simply theoretical dialogue that was deemed lacking but also a history; the other lament was that no text suggested ceramics had its own "historically coherent body of work."[4] This, too, seems irreconcilable with the publication of Garth Clark's large historical surveys, the (then named) American Craft Museum's centenary series, and numerous other durable contributions, from Cleota Reed's book on Henry Chapman Mercer through Ulysses Dietz's reevaluation of his own institution's history of collecting art pottery at the Newark Museum to Elaine Levin's wide-ranging survey that emerged in 1988 and Barbara Perry's numerous exhibitions. This has not stopped ceramicists from considering

1 Wayne Higby, foreword to Philip Rawson, *Ceramics*, 2nd ed. (Philadelphia: University of Pennsylvania Press, 1983), p. xv.
2 On November 10, 2012, Higby wrote me the following email: "Regarding my Rawson introduction, I was not referring to scholarly books in the field concerning the history of ceramic art or to Rawson's text.... Working artists are sensitive to the here and now. Is work being reviewed and, if so, are the reviews insightful?" I agree with his concerns here.
3 I conducted many interviews to frame and ponder these questions and especially thank George and Betty Woodman, Tony Hepburn, Jim Melchert, Neil Forrest, Del Harrow, and Jordan McDonald for their input and generosity.
4 Jeff Perrone, "Ceramic Criticism," *Ceramics Monthly* 33, no. 10 (December 1985), p. 28.

their field under-researched. As a bookish ceramophile who appreciated these publications, I wondered what fueled the perennial dismissal.

Even today these complaints endure, despite recent contributions such as Glenn Adamson's provocative *Thinking through Craft* (2010) and Edmund de Waal's *Twentieth-Century Ceramics* (2003). What is missing? The cheeky answer to this contradiction between plentiful publications and a dearth of intellectual debate might be that potters don't read, but an accompanying asterisk would need to explain why so many unhesitatingly fire off zealous rebuttals and keep the letters-to-the-editor page in ceramics periodicals at an emotional rolling boil.[5] Back in the 1980s, it was common for ceramicists to admit that among their brethren a rude "anti-intellectualism" prevented the production of good ceramic criticism. Janet Koplos opined that "lifestyle" remained more tangible a criterion in the field than any other ideal or theoretical construct; her view was both sympathetic and damning.[6]

A more courteous word for "lifestyle" might be ethos, understood to designate a working system and prevailing disposition. Conversations about clay between 1970 and the present exhibit remarkable consistency, hence the suitability and importance of such a term—ceramic discourse, even if lacking in criticality, can be said to have a particular character. My hypothesis is that the ethos of ceramics is worth probing in relation to this (mis)perception of an absence of critical discourse. I take ethos to be rooted in practice and discourse in linguistic framework.[7]

Prying open feisty discussions from a few decades ago, this essay tries to make sense of the printed word in ceramics in the 1980s and 1990s. The gist of the inquiry focuses on the practitioner as an exemplary scholar. At a conference in 1979, Higby made a plea for scholarship, arguing that "currently there are two major blocks to the successful rejuvenation of pottery as a primary expression." One of these was a "lack of knowledge about ceramic history" and the other was "misinterpretation" of Peter Voulkos's achievement. Ceramic history, stated Higby, "will tell you there is nothing new, but there is the possibility of rediscovery."[8] Voulkos's power had less to do with abstract painting, Higby argued, than with our attraction to similar artifacts, such as a magnificent Islamic urn. While Higby's prioritization of touch over sight is highly subjective, his argument has been consistent that materiality matters—and matters more than ever before. Higby's balancing act maintains both an aerial perspective of the field as well as that of one in the trenches—and this dual vision is his contribution.

The Artist as Scholar

One does not often hear of art historians arguing that artists produce research equally valuable to their own, but Ernst Gombrich risked such a proposal in his essay "Art and Scholarship."[9] More common is the declaration among artists that trucking too deeply in words or thoughts can capsize visual acumen. In other words, writing stifles artistic instinct. Scholars of American culture are more likely to associate the idea of "knowing by doing" with John Dewey's educational ideals than with Renaissance art history, but Gombrich identified the origins of the productive relationship between studio practice and historical inquiry in the multitalented and incredibly ambitious Vasari. In the arena of craft practice, Gombrich's idealization of tacit knowledge prevails—and is the normative seedbed for authentic production (despite the enormous number of how-to manuals published each year). Many crafts practitioners express conviction in their method—their subversion of the divided labor and large-scale production common in industrialization— with more cer-

1 Artist's studio, 2012. Alfred Station, New York.

tainty than they articulate the ways their productions impact the larger world in a positive fashion. This prevailing faith in materiality and practice falls within the sphere of ethos, not discourse.

In the six decades since Gombrich's essay appeared, artists have become an integral part of the university and an immense percentage of the professoriate class who publish and contribute to academic conferences. Vasari recuperated tempera in his practice as a painter, which had become an obsolete method; similarly Higby's decision to revive the use of techniques such as Egyptian paste can be seen as having an antiquarian instinct. Such material practice is cyclical more than it is cumulative, and often the knowledge is non-transferable even if the technique is inherited. But what is the value and circulation of contemporary practitioners' verbal contributions? Papers by teaching artists seem to drift oddly in a netherworld, not really becoming a proper self-reflective discourse and all the while growing in stature as legitimized research. Artists such as Donald Judd and Andrea Fraser are included in compendia of criticism about sculpture and museology, but practitioners working in craft-associated media are less frequently seen as thinkers. In American ceramics, verbal methods of teaching through explicit knowledge have been criticized and remain a minority approach. We have no seminal paper delivered by Peter Voulkos, Rudy Autio, Paul Soldner, Ken Price, or Ken Ferguson; each expressed skepticism toward traditional academic pedagogical methods. (It is worth noting that this is not the case in Britain, where David Pye's insights have been widely disseminated. Contemporary potters such as Edmund de Waal, Julian Stair, Alison Britton, and the late Emmanuel Cooper sustain vigorous criticism.) Wayne Higby's regular publications and lectures are an interesting middle ground in which to ruminate over where scholarship is and what it does.

One would expect Higby's foreword to locate him in precisely such a position, as a practitioner who is widely read. In it, Higby celebrated that Rawson had won the major battle: pots were declared to be complicated and articulations of complex thought and to have bypassed the sophomoric quandary of "is it art or isn't it?" He praised that Rawson's work was rooted in materiality and a search for transcendence. Ceramics is precisely that, a modernist study of materials and human agency. Rawson wrote in praise of universals. His notions of symbolic action had little investigation into cultural ethnography or vernacular distinctions. Gender was as clear cut as an anthropomorphic shape, not a postmodern pastiche embracing indeterminacy.

While Rawson's text sounds like a perfect fit for the practitioner's arsenal, its reception in the ceramics community was not unanimously positive. A reviewer in American Ceramics expressed the need for "a Cliff Notes version" and, in thuggishly meandering sentences, obnoxiously derided the book as "unreadable."[10] The reviewer, a potter known for publishing on techniques, concluded with a suggestion that is a paradigmatic example of ethos obstructing discourse: "We should read about pots only when we have nothing better to do." This anti-intellectual stance but buttressed with a romantic quotation, one from Rilke suggesting that ceram-

5 In particular, Jens Morrison's highly caffeinated epistolary production supplies ample historical texture. See "Criticism at Last," American Ceramics 5, no. 1 (1985), p. 7, where he recounts "the ritual of driving two thousand miles to NCECA, smoking, drinking and hooting til dawn. Getting sick in hotel elevators, trying to watch slide presentations after downing a pint of Jack Daniels, bathtubs of beer in the Hilton Hotel Executive Suite," and then concludes, "There is a tendency to lump ceramics into one big pile of kaka."

6 "Most clay criticism published in the last thirty years, for example, says more about lifestyle than it does about art." Janet Koplos, "Exercising the Critical Muscle," American Ceramics 4, no. 4 (1985), p. 50. Koplos reiterated this in 1999 at the Ceramics Millennium conference in Amsterdam; see "Ceramics and Art Criticism," in Ceramic Millennium, ed. Garth Clark (Halifax: NSCAD Press, 2006), p. 286.

7 Ethos has also been interpreted as in opposition to pathos, a polarization between ideal character and actual sentiment, but I use the term less to refer to the exegesis of Aristotle's Rhetoric than to common language. The more academically inclined might substitute the term hegemony for ethos, but such a word makes aesthetic debates a bit too rarified and wrought with the tensions of geopolitical antagonisms.

8 Wayne Higby, "Aesthetics," MSS, 1979.

9 Ernst Gombrich, "Art and Scholarship," College Art Journal 17, no. 4 (Summer 1958), pp. 342–56.

10 Jack Troy, "May Pots Survive Their Writers," American Ceramics 5, no. 1 (1985), p. 35.

ics "are inexpressible, taking place in a realm which no word has ever entered."[11] In hindsight, Higby's generosity towards the text and his ability to embrace Rawson's formal analysis and to articulate its particular contribution—the memory trace as a pot's window into deep time—were noteworthy. Others favored dreamy mysticism.

Higby continues to occupy a distinct role as one of the foremost practitioners who values verbal play and labor, historical reverie, and self-reflective criticism in addition to tacit knowledge, direct engagement with materiality, and the transcendent capabilities of process. These might seem like parallel streams that should naturally intersect but their integration in the crafts is uncommon. By his own recognition, Higby encountered hostility for his lectures. His preference for talking instead of demonstrating technique remains a minority approach. Go to the annual NCECA conference and one can spy a thousand people craning their necks to see a potter handling a wheel on stage, shaping a cylinder large enough to use as a sarcophagus. A caption in a publication recapping events at *Super Mud* in 1979 drew a comparison between "Higby talking" and another ceramist who used his time on stage to build a giant carrot. Higby remembers attending an NCECA in the 1980s and Paul Soldner sizing him up with the quip, "You're the intellectual one."[12] The backhanded compliment reveals an important shift in professional norms as well as personal tendencies. Higby had the ethos of honoring practice and materiality and yet sought to solidify a scholarly footing in academia.

The divide in the craft world between those who select to honor materiality and its history and those who refute that there is a distinct medium-specific aesthetic becomes palpable when reading Barbaralee Diamonstein's *Handmade in America: Conversations with Fourteen Craftmasters* (1983), in which interviews with Ron Nagle and Higby seemingly delineate a binary opposition in ceramics. The two interviews, when extracted together, stand as antitheses between reverence versus irreverence for ceramic tradition and history. Whereas Nagle embraces pop culture and cites Californian music and lifestyle as his primary influences, Higby genuflects to history broadly and declares his allegiance to Minoan pottery. Nagle resists fealty to the Japanese teacups he admits to owning and maintains that he springs forward in revolution to ceramic tradition. Higby owns up to having a "healthy sense of ego" but states that his work has an evolutionary relationship to the past. Nagle and Higby also neatly exemplify the binary opposition in craft between urban ephemerality and pastoral transcendence. Confusingly, each of these practitioners see themselves as embodying the fundamentals of modernism—one because he calls for revolt against tradition, and the other because he embraces the essence of his medium, a criterion of the "art of limitations."[13]

Higby praised boundaries to distinguish his own agenda from a doctrinaire modernism; his focus on clay and on the vessel were avowedly not reductive. In a 1982 lecture titled "The Vessel: Overcoming the Tyranny of Modern Art," Higby suggested "the modernist's idea of purity becomes life-denying. In contrast, the vessel is life-affirming."[14] A few years later, in the *Studio Potter*, he wrote:

> It is important to me that my work has been called innovative. However, I have been more concerned with becoming part of a continuum that reaches backward for thousands of years and yet has vitality in the present. Being a participant in the continuous evolution of pottery puts me in touch with a timeless symbolic language that speaks in support of my own personal quest for essential meanings.[15]

At that time, few used the term "modernisms" to articulate this type of seemingly contradictory resolution of temporal meaning. It is notable that Higby did not engage in historicist ornament, another significant artistic 1970s' strategy to subvert orthodox modernism. His deployment of formalism was nuanced and influenced by George Kubler, in whose work

Peruvian altarpieces, not contemporary art, were primary concerns. Higby welcomed the historian's framework in which to ponder art, but he returned to individual experience, imagination, and the studio process as the primary mixture out of which an artist forms herself/himself. The material and medium of clay was a limitation for Higby but also the very avenue through which he communed with "timeless symbolic language."

As George Woodman's student at the University of Colorado Boulder in the 1960s, Higby had encountered art history for the first time. Prior to that, he had enjoyed clay but not seen its broader role in history. He remembers being a student in an auditorium in morning lectures and getting to know Woodman more intimately later in a drawing class. Woodman's lectures and his efforts in bringing visitors like sculptor Manuel Neri to campus, who shared images of ceramic work by Henry Takemoto, Mason and Voulkos, stirred both passion and motivation. Higby read Gombrich and Lewis Mumford and gained Woodman as a lifelong friend, along with his wife Betty, who included Higby's work in a three-person show in 1965, alongside her own and that of Maria Martinez. In turn, he arranged Betty Woodman's first museum exhibition at the Joslyn Art Museum in Omaha. By his mid-twenties he was exhibiting in the Smithsonian in *Objects: USA* and publishing statements of his artistic intentions; ever since that time, his writing has developed alongside his career as an artist and teacher.

The Artist as Educator

I am not against talking or writing about art. My colleagues in Ceramic Art [at Alfred University] will bear witness to that. I enjoy words and philosophical discussion almost as much as making. As a university professor who has some influence on what undergraduate and graduate art students must accomplish, I have been an advocate for developing the skills of reflective criticism…. Criticism, Aesthetics and Art History are important elements of of an art curriculum [sic] at all levels, but they fall into place through making as an elemental priority.[16]

Because the twentieth century moved the ceramicist from vocational schools to liberal arts universities, subsequent makers have been given a tall order, a dual duty to argue on behalf of clay and also to seek legitimacy as humanist inquiry, and this explains Higby's hybrid position. In the field at large, the privileging of process was rarely tempered. Many academics oriented themselves to anti-academic as well as anti-intellectual positions, but Higby recoiled from biting the hand that fed him. He often asked students to write and saw it as an exercise that "forced you to organize your thoughts in a linear fashion." But students' writing was never a product to evaluate; Higby uses writing as a process to ask "how do you empower students?"

However, in a 1988 presentation at the Portland Museum of Art, he articulated an equally strong commitment to process. He stated that "too much intellectualization and deductive reasoning inhibits the potential for fully experiencing a work of art. It is best to simply receive the work and to accept willingly that it often cannot be trapped or held in the net of a rational way of knowing." Taken out of context, this could be considered an example of the ceramics ethos cutting off discourse, but Higby continued in his presentation to state that his final goal was communion, that ceramics "offers a physical-material bridge over which one may travel back and forth from a point of sensual reality to a point of abstract reverie."[17]

11 Ibid., p. 37.
12 Author's conversation with Wayne Higby, Alfred Station, April 24, 2012.
13 Garth Clark, *American Potters: The Work of Twenty Modern Masters* (New York: Watson-Guptill, 1981), p. 26. See Glenn Adamson, "Implications: The Modern Pot," in *Shifting Paradigms in Contemporary Ceramics*, eds. Garth Clark and Cindi Straus (New Haven/Houston: Yale University Press in association with the Museum of Fine Arts, Houston, 2012), pp. 36–45. See Glenn Adamson on the pastoral as a continuum in *Thinking through Craft* (Oxford: Berg, 2007), pp. 106–20.
14 Wayne Higby, "The Vessel: Overcoming the Tyranny of Modern Art," MSS, NCECA, 1982.
15 Wayne Higby, "Innovation: A Matter of Connections," *The Studio Potter* 12, no. 2 (June 1984).
16 Wayne Higby, "Making an Elemental Priority," MSS, NCECA, 1990.
17 In his lectures Higby also cited Howard Gardner, *Frames of Mind* (1983); Gaston Bachelard, *Poetics of Space* (1958); Tarmo Pasto, *The Space-Frame Experience in Art* (1964); and Buckminster Fuller, *Critical Path* (1981).

Coming to Alfred in 1973, Higby had already experienced the variegated roles of art education in Boulder and then at the University of Michigan, where he completed his graduate work, as well as in his first teaching positions at the University of Nebraska and also the Rhode Island School of Design. This trajectory and ultimate relocation was a part of Higby's positioning and repositioning in relation to material and process. At Alfred, ceramics had a long and complex history as applied art, art, industrial design, and craft but had mostly been closer to ceramic engineering than it was to the liberal arts. Moreover, the territorialization of ceramics between East and West in the 1960s and 1970s is palpable when reading Rose Slivka and other critics in *Craft Horizons* or *Ceramics Monthly*; Higby was going establishment. He joined a faculty that itself was largely composed of Alfred graduates, where he was at first an outsider. But Higby also perceived that the old-fashioned Alfred vessel was losing respect in the 1970s, and his introduction of landscape and subject matter was one way to argue that art pottery had a conceptual conceit. The "classic Alfred pot" was a strong form with a complex glaze, and Higby struck some colleagues as an *enfant terrible* for wanting it to be more ambitious. Higby described his bowls as "wheel-thrown and *corrected*" (my italics). The wheel was a mere tool; the artist turned a pot into art.

Balancing vocational commitment and artistic ambition, Higby's statements for juried exhibitions in the 1970s strive to legitimate ceramics as an intellectual process. In 1976, at the Museum of Contemporary Art, Chicago, he claimed that "craft is an area of specialization that deals principally with ideas." Alfred was the "guardian of established values," in the view of his former colleague Tony Hepburn.[18] Hepburn remembers pushing back against the dedication to materiality at Alfred during his tenure between 1974 and 1993. He tried to be provocative by calling Higby "the protector of the faith." Both men shared the common aim of raising artistic ambition, but Higby articulated his intense loyalty to the materiality of clay overtly.

Higby himself saw his role at Alfred as that of a provocateur, too. In 1999, he wrote that "throughout the twentieth century Alfred has been a force, a contender, a catalyst, a protagonist and yes, perhaps even, at times a sleepy giant exhausted from the rigors of success and drowsy from the drug of self-importance."[19] Here, the artist looked back in the rearview mirror after nearly three decades of teaching and saw cycles of dynamic growth and subsequent fallow periods. It was an admission that institutions are dependent on criticism as much as they are prone to the vagaries of crop rotation.

2   Wayne Higby with his students. Sculpture II class, School of Art and Design, Alfred University, Alfred, New York, 2012.

The Craftsman as Author

Ego was both a danger that Higby warned others to be wary of and also a necessity in order to be artistically successful. In his 1985 essay titled "Craft as Attitude," he mourned that "careerism has replaced the search for the unknown," questioned the validity of art schools, and decried the ways pots were made to look good for photographs. Marketing and self-promotion were a problem in the crafts, he stated unequivocally. Higby's critique of the feverish marketplace and the pressures of commodification is a text worth revisiting—and comparing to Garth Clark's widely-disseminated 2010 lecture "How Envy Killed the Crafts" at the Portland Museum of Contemporary Craft. Clark's attack on studio craft aspiring to the price tag of fine art was not new. In 1980, Higby readily identified the problem when he faulted "Michael Lucero [who] seems to have yielded to a world of fashionable 'high art.'"[20] Higby also stated more fully the rationale for such a sea change in the first place, making his essay a bit more useful than Clark's indictment. Looking back at the 1970s in 1985, Higby thought art-making became preferable to craft-making for many, including himself, because "for many intelligent and highly creative individuals the duplicity of the art world looked better than the banality of the macramé pot hanger."[21] Higby's account implicates his own agency (another tidbit Garth Clark leaves out of his narrative) and fleshes out the contradiction wherein craft driven by lifestyle feels the tug of craftsmanship aspiring to be fine art. Higby also quoted his colleague Robert Turner's ideal of "integration." "Craft as an attitude is an approach to art and life in which integrity and pursuit of excellence are synonymous," he wrote.[22] This was another way to navigate the tension caused by career ambitions. Could the artist have an ego and still aspire to emulate Yanagi's "Unknown Craftsman"?

The tension between these ideals and the tug of materialism—in clay as a medium-specific commitment and in ambition as a barometer of artistic success—can be succinctly grasped by interpretations of Zen and its importance in the late-twentieth-century craft world. Higby often quoted the Chinese Zen proverb in explaining "in order to paint bamboo one must become bamboo."[23] Higby expanded upon this notion of sentient materiality when he admitted that "I've always thought of working with clay as a kind of collaboration. Clay has a mind of its own.... You have to get in on its wavelength and make your moves at the right time in order to accomplish your objectives." Yet even colleagues like Philip Rawson, who shared these ideals, saw a dilemma at hand. "Where there is ambition, there is no Zen," wrote Rawson in 1990, refuting the transcendence of the highly individualized artistic vessel.[24] Rawson took comfort increasingly in the past as he aged, and repudiated many contemporary vessels as spiritually "empty," even as his formal studies had encouraged the very same ceramicists to believe that by fusing the lips of a Chinese cup and the spout of a Cycladic ewer they could sustain a lifetime of "inexhaustible forms."[25] For the living ceramicist who wanted to be productive, Rawson's diagnosis was impossible to believe of oneself—even if it was directed at others.

The 1987 spat between Warren MacKenzie and Higby in the pages of *Ceramics Monthly* makes tangible this *fin-de-siècle* condition, the crisis between artistic authorship and anonymous craftsmanship. Higby's concept of artistic creation contrasted with MacKenzie's. Higby argued for dispensing with utility: "I do believe that functional pottery restricts freedom of expression."[26] With considerable vitriol, MacKenzie ridiculed the notion that Higby made "pots about pots," as if this self-reflective process were intellectually self-serving. In 1990, the two came head to head again when they assessed ceramics in the collection of the Nelson-Atkins

18   Conversation with author, May 24, 2012.

19   Wayne Higby, "Legend of Alfred," MSS, 1999, p. 2.

20   Wayne Higby, "Young Americans in Perspective," *American Craft* 42, no. 2 (April–May 1980), p. 22.

21   Wayne Higby, "Craft as Attitude," Haystack Mountain School of Crafts symposium mss., August 1985.

22   Ibid.

23   Wayne Higby, "Drawing as Intelligence," *The Studio Potter* 14, no. 1 (December 1985), pp. 36–37.

24   Philip Rawson, "Ceramic Overview," in *Recent Fires: Contemporary American Ceramics* (Salt Lake City: Utah Museum of Fine Arts, 1990), p. 3.

25   Philip Rawson, "Empty Vessels," *Ceramics Monthly* 34, no. 7 (September 1986), p. 55.

26   Wayne Higby, Letter to the Editor, *Ceramics Monthly* 35, no. 4 (April 1987), p. 7.

Museum of Art and published their choices in the pages of *Ceramics Monthly*.[27] Higby's breadth of appreciation across continents was in stark contrast to MacKenzie's limited palette of Asian pots. And the primitivism espoused by MacKenzie is a bit shocking to contemporary eyes. He regretted that "our culture does not dispose us to thinking like a Korean potter of old." The tension I am describing lay overtly in MacKenzie's sense of a path into the future: he denied a standard and encouraged potters to develop their individual intuition but also idealized pots with "no sense of ego in any of them." How are these to be balanced? The cul-de-sac of the honest/modest pot was in clear contrast to the highway of freedom that Higby set out, a pluralist view of the past intended to match the heterogeneity of the present.

But Higby did not advocate total freedom at the expense of losing touch with the medium of clay or the ceramic tradition. In celebrating the vessel as an extension of ceramic history into modernist art, Higby neared drafting a manifesto:

> The contemporary vessel must express the irreducible dynamics of pottery, but remain outside the realm of function. When the possibility of use enters into the vessel equation, the pure formal essence of the pot is altered to accommodate practical considerations that inevitably restrict the artist's freedom. A pot that is neither a vessel nor a functional object will lack definitive presence and create confusion in the viewer's mind.[28]

Too much hybridity was a bad thing. On this, Higby, Rawson, and Clark all agreed, with the latter two resorting to macho sexual metaphors in their prose. Rawson saw the growing interest in surface ornament and attendant diminished concern with sculptural volume as "sensuous castration."[29] Clark saw such in-between pots that hadn't the sea legs to stand as sculpture as "grotesquely androgynous" artifice.[30] In these ways, the artist stood shoulder to shoulder with the authors of ceramic criticism of his day.

In the 1980s, there were several summits asking from which source criticism might come. *Studio Potter* published a 1980 NCECA panel on which Tony Hepburn, George Woodman, and Warren MacKenzie opined.[31] *Ceramics Monthly* and *American Ceramics* followed suit, but little consensus was achieved about what form ceramic criticism would take. Rawson was the writer whose book most ceramicists quoted, largely to elucidate their intention. For MacKenzie, philosophy and lifestyle were ineluctably intertwined. In contrast, Woodman was an elegant and purposeful writer whose range made *Studio Potter* more intellectually engaging than the glossier periodicals. The breadth of interests he and others staked out went well beyond the periodical's name.[32]

Higby drew away from Clark and Rawson and neared MacKenzie's ethos in his conviction that each artist (and student) should start from their self as a starting point, and that such a ground zero might be a foundation for heroic studio production. Clark urged the living artist to start with a sense of contemporaneity and an ear to the current art scene. Rawson suggested that one commune with historical solutions to replenish form and meaningfulness. Higby, repeating a comment by Lee Nordness, believed that the American artist should aspire to be a transcendentalist, such as Henry Thoreau, instead of an inventor, such as Leonardo da Vinci.[33] Ethos wins out; his fundamental motivation for making lies in becoming and being.

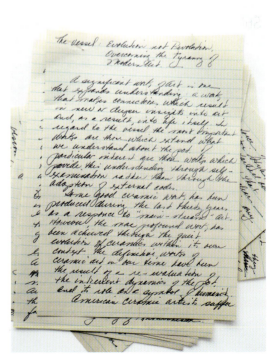

3   Original first draft text for the 1982 essay "The Vessel: Overcoming the Tyranny of Modern Art."

Higby's idealization of the innocent artist and the purity of materiality resonates in the pantheon of American protagonists who navigate both cultivation and the frontier.[34] R. W. B. Lewis described this Edenic rhetoric as one way to negotiate modernity. Lewis cites Ralph Waldo Emerson clamoring, "Here's for the plain old Adam, the simple genuine self against the whole world." With this ethos, the potter yearned for the preindustrialized state and climbed the heights of a fully industrialized postwar nation. Craft appeared to be a road away from homogenization and indulgent consumption. A pot stood in opposition to the United States' military industrial complex, even if kaolin mining, the aluminum wheel, and glaze ingredients were all by-products of this system.

Ethos or Discourse?

Today, practitioners still perceive themselves as engaging authenticity whether they have advanced degrees such as an MFA or not; the chase toward innocent creativity continues in craft. Witness Faythe Levine's *Handmade Nation* (2008), a documentary showing that the goal to assemble the signs and floating signifiers of mass culture into a new and highly contrived folk culture seems to be widespread. The promise that individuality can be achieved by forming raw or semi-processed materials persists, as well as the dream that such individuality can be preserved. The binary opposition between so-called honest functional pottery and expressive artistic sculpture remains current in American craft too; these still resurface in distinct, splintered, and often regional communities. Often these groups are polarized by lifestyle. In our sub-urban nation, the distinctions between the pastoral and urban are often more imagined than hard and fast, and they are still powerful as perceptions. The categorical distinction between belonging to craft or design as an identity also chugs along.

The persistence of an ethos does not mean that we cannot pause to ponder R. W. B. Lewis's identification of Walt Whitman as willfully naïve and still celebrate the poet and his poems. Or does it? In returning to look at the 1980s, I am struck by the similar way that the ceramics community felt snubbed by the Whitney Museum's *Ceramic Sculpture: Six Artists* in 1981 for the same reasons that the Institute of Contemporary Art's *Dirt on Delight* enflamed passions more recently in 2009: there was the sense that the makers' relationship to materiality and ownership of clay was not respected. Still today, ceramicists grapple over whether they want to be identified as artists or clayworkers first, and whether their art be seen primarily or secondarily as clay. It is worth pondering if the ethos of material identification might preclude the development of a complex theoretical discourse.

This essay is a tribute to the ways Wayne Higby has conducted himself as an artist and scholar with as much gravity and thoughtfulness as any critic or historian, labored with empathy and pragmatism toward the past. He has evaded the dogmas of his era. Perhaps Gombrich deserves the concluding thought, if only to honor the ideal artist who is a critically perceptive agent and is truly culturally engaged with pasts as well as the future: "If there is anyone in need of undistorted memories it is the artist in our world."[35]

27 Wayne Higby and Warren MacKenzie, "Potters' Choice," *Ceramics Monthly* 38, no. 3 (March 1990), pp. 53–59.
28 Wayne Higby, "The Vessel is Like a Pot," *American Ceramics* 3, no. 4 (April 1985).
29 Rawson 1990 (see note 24).
30 Clark 1981 (see note 13), p. 23.
31 See "Aesthetics, Criticism and the Arts," *The Studio Potter* 8, no. 1 (December 1980), pp. 68–73.
32 For instance, see "In Search of a Unified Theory of Craft," *The Studio Potter* 23, no. 1 (December 1994), pp. 1–17.
33 Higby 1985 (see note 21).
34 R. W. B. Lewis, *The American Adam: Innocence, Tragedy, and Tradition in the Nineteenth Century* (Chicago: University of Chicago Press, 1955).
35 Gombrich 1958 (see note 9).

LACUNA ROCK, 1999. Glazed earthenware, raku-fired. 8 × 8 × 5¼ inches. Private collection

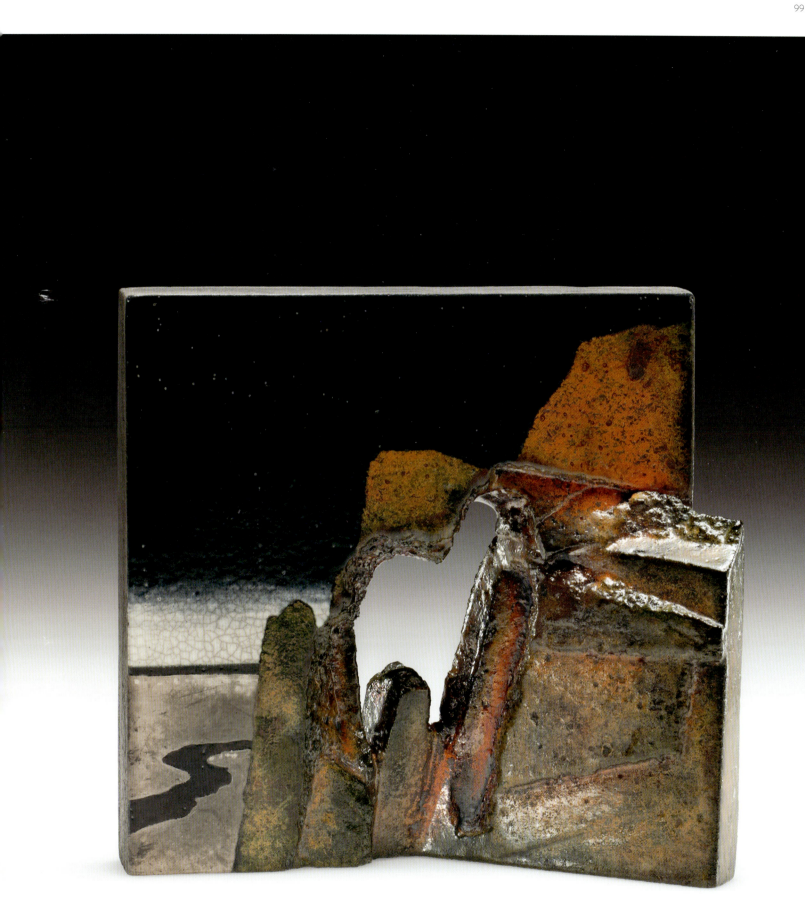

37   EVENTIDE BEACH, 1990. Glazed earthenware, raku-fired. 14 × 15¾ × 2¼ inches. Collection of the artist
38   GREEN RIVER GORGE, 2002. Glazed earthenware, raku-fired. 9 × 9½ × 3½ inches. Private collection

39   STONE GATE, 2007. Glazed earthenware, raku-fired. 14½ × 16 × 6 inches. Collection of the artist
40   EIDOLON CREEK, 2002. Glazed earthenware, raku-fired. 8 × 11 × 4½ inches. Private collection

INTANGIBLE NOTCH, 1995. Glazed earthenware, raku-fired. 11 feet × 10 feet × 13 inches. Commission for Arrow International, Reading, Pennsylvania

41 INTANGIBLE NOTCH, 1995 (details)

LAKE POWELL MEMORY—CLIFFS III, 1995. Glazed porcelain. 15 × 17 × 19 inches. Collection: Marlin and Regina Miller

43   LAKE POWELL CLIFFS, 1994. Ink, brush on newsprint. 14 × 17 inches. Collection of the artist
42   LAKE POWELL MEMORY—CLIFFS III, 1995 (detail)

44   CANYON LAKE 1, 1994. Black marker on paper. 7 × 9 inches. Collection of the artist
45   CANYON LAKE 2, 1994. Ink, brush on newsprint. 14 × 17 inches. Collection of the artist
46   LAKE POWELL MEMORY—SEVEN MILE CANYON, 1996. Glazed porcelain. 16¾ × 22 × 10 inches. Collection: Los Angeles County Museum of Art, California

47   LAKE POWELL MEMORY—STONE POOL, 1998. Glazed porcelain. 15 × 18 × 7½ inches. Collection: Helen W. Drutt English
48   LAKE POWELL MEMORY—RECOLLECTION FALLS, 1996. Glazed porcelain. 16½ × 20 × 9 inches. Private collection

49 LAKE POWELL MEMORY—WINTER RAIN, 1998. Glazed porcelain. 16¾ × 22¾ × 9½ inches. Collection: Smithsonian American Art Museum, Washington, D.C.

An Auspicious Alignment: Wayne Higby and China

CARLA COCH

1 Zhu Danian and Wayne Higby at the Beijing International Ceramic Art Convention, 1991.

Scenes along the River during the Qingming Festival, a famous Northern Song dynasty handscroll measuring seventeen feet by four inches, freeze-frames a panoramic moment on an early April day in the city now known as Kaifeng. At the outset, a solitary herdsman traverses an unmarked path as he heads toward a rickety bridge. Likewise, Wayne Higby first entered China in the spring of 1991 without a map. His journey of nearly two-and-a-half decades begins, as does the scroll, amid unpeopled thickets and moves to the urban square—from wilderness to community. A letter inviting him to teach at the Central Academy of Fine Arts (CAFA) said presciently, "In your work, you do have something in common with the Chinese scholar's spiritual world."[1] No one then, perhaps not even he himself, could have imagined how deeply he would explore that world or how immensely his commitment to China would come to matter.

In Beijing, Higby gave slideshows of his life in Alfred, his work, and the art program at the New York School of Art and Design at Alfred University (AU). Momentarily disconcerted by students photographing all his slides, he quickly realized how hungry young Chinese artists were for images of contemporary ceramics practiced in the Western studio potter tradition. He sensed their urgency and their excitement on the cusp of their country's entry into a global arena in economics and the arts. China, he sensed intuitively, was on the threshold of a singularity.

At the BICAC conference[2] Higby was particularly inspired by the slideshow of porcelain master Zhu Danian, who called upon artists to understand their materials and their history (fig. 1). China's ceramic tradition, he said, looking to both past and future, is "a fundamental platform for risk and adventure."[3] Higby reformulated this concept as a question: "How can artists in China be open to as well as benefit from a world of ideas and information while simultaneously remaining true to that deep resonance of what it means to be Chinese?"[4] Ultimately, real change always comes from within, but as a teacher and artist, he has brought knowledge from without for many young ceramists in China, transformed the pedagogy, and inspired new ways of seeing and making.

In Beijing, Higby met many artists from Jingdezhen, China's ancient porcelain capital, four of whom remain his close friends to this day: sculptors Zhou Guozhen and Yao Yongkang, painter and eventual president of Jingdezhen Ceramic Institute (JCI), Qin Xilin and Li Jiansheng (known as Jackson Lee). The collaboration between Wayne Higby and Jackson Lee, in particular, has been responsible for exponential growth in exchanges between China and Alfred, China and the world.

From the very beginning—and little diminished thereafter—Higby has said yes to requests for official letters of invitation for Chinese ceramists to come to the United States, for him to lecture and teach in China, and for his help facilitating all manner of international activities. For example, he has secured scholarships and jobs for ceramicists in China and the United States, arranged itineraries for visitors coming and going, and conducted countless interviews both here and in China where few contemporary Western artists had previously been featured in the media.

The following year, 1992, at the Hubei Academy of Fine Arts (HAFA) in Wuhan, Higby saw firsthand how China's educational system emphasized imitation over innovation, conformity over creativity. "Questioning and individual think-

1 Zheng Tang, letter to Wayne Higby, August 9, 1991.
2 BICAC stands for Beijing International Ceramic Art Convention. At the invitation of Taiwan American ceramicist Lee Mao-chung, Higby attended with Arne Ase (Norway), James D. Makins (USA), Ann Mortimer (Canada), Nino Caruso (Italy), and Ronald A. Kuchta (USA). The convention was sponsored by the United Nations Development Program and held at North China University of Technology.
3 Zhu Danian, closing address at the BICAC lecture, China, April 19, 1991.
4 Wayne Higby, "Masters of American Ceramics: The New Generation," keynote address at the Jingdezhen Kaolin International Art Conference, Jingdezhen, China, August 1, 1995.

2   Wayne Higby and close friend, scholar Mao Jianxiong, Guangzhou, 2000.

ing so celebrated in my art school seems quite absent from the curriculum," he wrote.[5] For more than two decades, his energies have been dedicated to overcoming that deficit.

Before the Internet and cell phones, communication between China and the West was complicated: garbled faxes, peculiar translations, and missed long-distance calls. Further frustrations included visas denied, funds withheld, projects shelved, tepid institutional support, and ambivalence toward China in general. Nonetheless, Higby was not disheartened; rather, he advanced resolutely in the manner of the stream-crossing traveler of Chinese lore who must toss ahead one stone at a time in order to secure the next step. With grace and good humor, he has navigated minefields of culture shocks, such as protocols, "face," and hierarchies. His full-time teaching and art career meant he usually had to go to China in the summers where wilting heat, over-stuffed trains, no-star accommodations, and hazardous transportation made traveling there challenging, particularly in the early 1990s when foreigners were not permitted to use Chinese currency and might be under surveillance in areas unfrequented by tourists.

Immediately after that first encounter with China, Higby immersed himself in the scholarly study of Chinese philosophy, dynastic history, art, and cultural and spiritual practices, most recently in Buddhism. His home in Alfred, New York, is full of paintings, sculptures, and textiles brought back from his trips to East Asia, but most noticeably, it overflows with books—heaped and piled everywhere. During his 1993 sabbatical year, he wrote to a friend in China, "This year, I have not been at my school. I spend all my time working in my studio trying to understand porcelain and brush and ink drawing. I think I am becoming Chinese."[6]

In 1992, Higby and his wife Donna spent five weeks touring major cities in China. Wherever he went he gave a talk, a slide show, a workshop, a demo—including a three-hour presentation for Liu Yuanchang's artisans employed at Jing-dezhen's Sculpture Factory. In 1994, he and Jackson Lee traveled to cities with major art universities, where he continued his robust schedule of giving slideshows and teaching classes. At each step along his trajectory, what came to be called "the China dialogue" expanded.

In the same year in Guangzhou, Higby first met Mao Jianxiong, art history professor at South China Normal University, who was soon to become a close friend and traveling companion (fig. 2). Professor Mao said Wayne's first words to him were, "Are you interested in teaching in the US?"[7] In typical fashion, Higby used his connections to arc synapses that subsequently sparked their own outcomes. Alfred University MFA graduate Benjamin DeMott alluded to this gift when he praised his teacher's "sensitivity to get people together," adding that he knows how to build trust among team members and "sees possibilities in them and their skill sets."[8]

Mao Jianxiong describes Higby as his "spiritual brother." Like literati scholars of old, they spend their time together discussing Chinese philosophy, religion, aesthetics, and the like, while traveling to distant places such as Tibet, Dunhuang, Yunnan, and Heilongjiang. "He raises questions quietly," Professor Mao said. "He listens so hard, and when there is a point of contention, he is the one to help to bring about a peaceful result."[9]

5   Wayne Higby, summary narrative of trip to HAFA, 1992.
6   Wayne Higby, letter to HAFA professor Xie Yue, February 2, 1994.
7   Mao Jianxiong, telephone interview, October 26, 2011.
8   Benjamin DeMott, personal interview, June 4, 2012.
9   Mao Jianxiong, telephone interview, October 26, 2011.
10   Walter Ostrom, telephone interview, January 10, 2012.
11   Yao Yongkang, personal interview, trans. Huang Chunmao, October 21, 2011.
12   Wayne Higby, private notebook entry, May 20, 1994.

Also in 1994, the idea for an artists' residency modeled after the Haystack Mountain School of Crafts in Maine where Higby is a Life Trustee was hatched. Four years later, near the village of Sanbao, about five miles south of Jingdezhen, the dream began to become a reality when Jackson Lee oversaw the transformation of a rammed-earth farmhouse into a rustic studio (fig. 3). Today, he, his sister Li Wenying (Wendy) and her husband Mei Jianxiang, and Higby have made San-bao a destination for creative people from all over the world—a joyful gathering place with galleries, a museum, a restaurant, and a teahouse rebuilt from Ming dynasty timbers. It accommodates more than twenty-five guests and meanders along the hillside where the ancient, soothing sound of water-powered trip hammers still echoes down the valley.

In 1995, Higby was asked to invite three guests to join him in China. He chose Walter Ostrom, ceramicist and teacher at Nova Scotia College of Art and Design (NSCAD), Xavier Toubes from the Netherlands, and Toni Sikes, proprietor of guild.com, an online market featuring fine art for the home. In 2001, he curated a gallery for her website, which gave Westerners their first opportunity to see—and own—the fine-arts porcelain still being made in Jingdezhen today.

With his vast slide library and ebullient teaching style, Ostrom was a most fortunate addition to the retinue. Were it not for Higby, he affirmed, the whole enterprise would never have gotten off the ground. He calls him "the most important factor in China's opening up to world ceramics, especially to North American clay artists."[10] An ambassador, pioneer, and catalyst ever present in China "emotionally and intellectually," according to Ostrom, he has the tenacity to stay focused and the charisma to bring others along with him.

In Jingdezhen, Yao Yongkang recalls an especially memorable class that his friend taught for his third-year sculpture students (fig. 4). First, Higby invited everyone, teachers and students alike, to collaborate on making a piece. Instantly, constraints of rank and authority disappeared as students were given permission to play, to ask "what if", to have fun. Initially, the group created an oversized pyramid of clay, and then one by one, each student took turns changing it. The first person added a nose, the next a mouth, and so on—eventually down to the eyebrows. When it was his turn, Professor Yao slashed the edge of the mound, fashioned a slab, and stuck it onto the form, a gesture followed by Wayne's equally outside-the-box alteration.[11] Such exercises are commonplace in Western art schools, but not so in China where "the idea of serious play, experimentation, exploration [with] no end product" was anathema.[12]

Another crescendo of activity took place in 1998 when Higby and Jackson Lee led a two-bus tour to Yixing, famous for its exquisite hand-paddled teapots and for the first International Yixing Ceramic Art Conference. China had never heretofore hosted a conference that had brought so many international ceramicists and curators together. The tour continued on to Jingdezhen where Higby gave opening and closing remarks for the newly-launched summer school at JCI and celebrated Sanbao's dedication with the burial of a time capsule—and a party.

Along the entire length of Higby's China road, parties erupted—celebratory, raucous, karaoke-laden, toast-fueled

3   Wayne Higby and Jackson Lee at the farmer's house where the dream of Sanbao began, Jingdezhen, 1998.

extravaganzas where his magnetism drew people instantly into his circle. He hosted several such events himself, the first one in May 1994, in Jingdezhen. A party means music which means dancing, and dance is a fundamental language that overcomes all barriers. With wry understatement, he wrote a note to himself after a blow-out party at Sanbao: "We danced—wow."[13] When asked what it is like to travel with his friend, Mao Jianxiong told several hilarious anecdotes wherein Wayne spontaneously broke into dance—ballroom, free-form, the tango—whenever he heard street music or discovered people enjoying boom box-accompanied dance fests in public parks. Alfred University MFA graduate Li Hongwei recorded a memory of a New Year's Eve party in 2009 in Foshan, which over 200 factory workers helped celebrate: "Wayne danced with them, took pictures with them. I truly felt he had a very open mind, just like the ocean."[14]

In 2000, pandemonium and paparazzi accompanied the first International Ceramics Wood Firing Conference in Foshan, when Higby and his team brought Japanese American raku techniques to China for the first time. He tossed hot vessels into the air and sent sparks flying during the all-night firing spectacle enjoyed by over 500 people. As usual, he handled the celebrity spotlight with circumspection and equanimity. In China, he could always delight audiences with his showmanship or move them to tears with his eloquence.

Later that May in Jingdezhen, in his keynote address entitled "The Spirit of Porcelain," Higby credited his fellow artists in China who have "in a wonderful, mysterious way given me permission to work in porcelain." He described the "sensual and celestial qualities of the material"[15] in which he has worked almost exclusively for the past fifteen years. Recently, Yao Yongkang praised him for choosing celadon glazes for his large-scale architectural works. Redolent of mountains and water, "celadon is efficient," Professor Yao maintains, "a reflection of the Chinese scholar's mind with which Wayne has a deep affinity."[16] Compelling as it is to think about how China has affected his art, it is equally so to ponder how China has transformed his soul. At the halfway mark of *Scenes along the River during the Qingming Festival*, a boat at the head of a large flotilla prepares to pass under the Rainbow Bridge. The scene is chaotic, cacophonous, even perilous as the mast is hastily dropped, and the stern seems about to slam into the abutment. Adding to the mayhem, people crowd along the entire span of the arch; some toss towropes to oarsmen below and others gesticulate excitedly as if shouting out advice.

Well into his China adventures, Higby chose adjectives appropriate to the havoc pending at the Rainbow Bridge: "Complex and at times bewildering," he wrote, adding, "there is a sense of uncertainty."[17] He reiterates his hopes for Chinese artists to have greater access to studio resources and opportunities to express themselves freely. Unsure of the success of his decade-long efforts in China, he wrote, "10 to 20 years down the road—small opportunities may lead to solid results. Patience."[18] Looking back, the "dialogue" he initiated had already grown into a giant switchboard of conversations and self-propelled networks, including independent educational exchange programs at the University of West Virginia, NSCAD,

4   Wayne Higby teaching Yao Yongkang's sculpture class, Jingdezhen Ceramic Institute, 1994.

and SUNY Cortland. The following decade until today has seen Higby direct the majority of his energies in China to educational endeavors in Beijing and factory-based ones in Tangshan and Foshan.

In May 2004, Jingdezhen launched its millennial year celebrating 1,000 years since the Jingde reign mark was first brushed onto a porcelain vessel. At a gala banquet, Higby was named Honorary Citizen of Jingdezhen, the first Westerner to be so recognized. In a letter expressing gratitude for the honor, he called Jingdezhen "a maker's city," which "beckons all into the world of understanding that lies deep in material and process. Anyone who has found poetry and truth within skilled transformations of the earth will find Jingdezhen to be one of the greatest cities of the world."[19]

5   Wayne Higby with students and his staff at the Central Academy of Fine Arts, Beijing, 2005.

That same month, Higby met with Pan Gongkai, president of CAFA, to begin to hammer out details for an educational exchange program between AU and CAFA's City Design School. Developed over several years, the AU-CAFA model offers neither supplementary nor parallel programs; instead, it ensures integrated curricula and mutual understanding of each other's institutional goals (figs. 5, 6). In "The Spirit of Porcelain," Higby wrote, "We are now building more than a bridge. We are doing something more than connecting two distant points. We are constructing a permanent foundation upon which we will place a new structure—an architecture designed for the future—architecture of good will, mutual support, and collaboration."[20] Officially dedicated in January 2008, the AU-CAFA program makes manifest that vision.

More recently, an unexpected syzygy occurred in the southern China tile-making city of Foshan, where Higby met the young entrepreneur Chen Manjian (Ajian), proprietor of Individuality Art Ceramics, whose factory was used for Higby to fabricate his work in China for the first time. Over the course of a year, he and his team fashioned the sparkling, color-saturated tiles suspended on the wall of the Miller Performing Arts Center located in Reading, Pennsylvania.[21] Entitled *SkyWell Falls*, the installation depicts a waterfall, what he calls, "a meditation on the nature of impermanence" in the exhibition catalogue where he connects Zen philosophy with a longstanding sensibility, that is, how he "intuitively understood abstraction in Chinese art long before I fully comprehended it in Western artistic practice and many years before I first went to China."[22]

Statistics about Higby's alignment with China confirm the magnitude of his impact: sponsorship of five AU MFA graduates from Jingdezhen and Beijing; AU art residencies for six visiting Chinese ceramists, ten official delegations hosted in Alfred, eight keynote addresses launching major international conferences, and four honorary professorships. Of greatest significance, however, are the visits to China he has facilitated for hundreds of artists, students, curators, and researchers whose journey to the historical center of ceramics he has directly made possible.

Advancing relationships between the United States and China is but a part of Higby's mission, which is truly international in scope. As council member and then vice-president of the International Academy of Ceramics (IAC)

13   Wayne Higby, private notebook entry, May 18, 1998.

14   Li Hongwei, e-mail to author, January 28, 2012.

15   Wayne Higby, "The Spirit of Porcelain," keynote address at the Jingdezhen Ceramic Art Conference, May 27, 2000.

16   Yao Yongkang, personal interview, trans. Jin Wenwei, October 19, 2011.

17   Wayne Higby, "Lu Bin: Making as Intelligence," *Kerameiki techni: International Ceramic Art Review* 37 (April 2001), p. 64.

18   Wayne Higby, private notebook entry, August 1, 1995.

19   Wayne Higby, letter to Jingdezhen Party Secretary Xu Aimin, September 6, 2004.

20   Wayne Higby 2000 (see note 15).

21   *SkyWell Falls* is a permanent installation at Reading Area Community College, Reading, Pennsylvania, made possible by Marlin and Regina Miller.

22   Wayne Higby, "The Story of SkyWell Falls," in Wayne Higby, *SkyWell Falls* (Alfred, N.Y.: Higby, 2011), pp. 17, 19.

6   Alfred-CAFA Ceramic Design for Industry program studio, Central Academy of Fine Arts, Beijing, 2007.

he has used its platform to tell the world about what is happening in China. Most notably, his 2002 commissioned lecture "Uncharted Territory: Contemporary Chinese Ceramics— A Fourth Generation" delivered in Athens, Greece, gave IAC members the opportunity to learn about the cutting-edge art coming out of China after its belated opening up to the West. In talks at National Council on Education for the Ceramic Arts symposia, the Clay Studio in Philadelphia, and other venues, he further shared his insights concerning the extraordinary explosion in creativity he has both witnessed and hands-on inspired.

Higby's lectures have been heard by thousands of people, but he has reached his largest audience through his writings. In addition to his published lectures, he has written six articles about individual Chinese ceramicists, eight prefaces and introductions, ten articles in major Western periodicals, and two books about his work and China's influence on it. By speaking and writing, he continues to tell the story of that implosion whose nascent energy was so palpable to him in Beijing in 1991.

One particularly resonant metaphor Higby explores is the idea of "the space between," an analog for areas untouched by the brush so important to the metaphysics of Chinese painting. Never empty but "alive with potential, embracing doubt," this space is the locus where "past and future are brought together" to "nurture the imagination." He continued, "It is the nature of the artist to bridge the space between things—to bring together information in unexpected ways—in ways others cannot imagine."[23]

For his keynote address in Xi'an for the 2008 IAC biennial conference, Higby offered a comprehensive critique of those early years. Looking forward, he speculated about where Chinese art is headed in a digital world and global economy. He expressed the hope that young artists who have "yet to yearn for what is lost" will keep asking the question he posed nearly twenty years before: "How can Chinese ceramics become more modern without losing its Chinese character?"[24]

In a 1994 letter to his friend, Jingdezhen sculptor Zhou Guozhen cited an oft-quoted phrase attributed to Sun Tze that reads in pinyin as "tianshi dili renhe." "Possessing the will of heaven," it can be translated, "the resources of the earth, and harmony among people in between, nothing is impossible." The simplified version asserts that "success depends upon the right time, place, and people." Among the three things, harmonious human relationships are always the most important. When asked what he treasures most from his long engagement with China, Higby unhesitatingly answers that it is the people—or more specifically, those moments of psychic connection beyond words when profound, transcendent understanding takes place.

Times and places in China—Higby has experienced so many: resplendent temples and serene monasteries, sublime landscapes, ice sculptures in Harbin, snow-sweepers in Pingyao, rain falling slant-wise on cliff faces along the Yangtze River, and many, many more. He can bring each to life in words and photographs, but all are secondary to what he most cherishes: communion between people who share their art and humanity deep in the bones.

In a recent poignant interview, Yao Yongkang illustrated his take on this kind of synergy. First, he gently unwrapped the two gifts—both small enough to be carried easily—that Wayne had given him: one, a rock-shaped form, and the other, a jagged white object that would, in Higby's upcoming architectural installations, be fashioned into a cloud. Each was a synecdoche of his friend's work—not where he had been, but where he was going. Wayne "has been touched by the flame … and carries the weight of the culture into his work," said Professor Yao (fig. 7).[25] Then, his frail health notwithstanding, ever so slowly, reverently, he brought the piece to his lips.

7   Yao Yongkang and Wayne Higby in Jingdezhen.

The finale of *Scenes along the River during the Qingming Festival* takes place in the vibrant city center thronged with merchants, traders, and makers. It celebrates the kind of thriving community that Higby has dedicated so many steps in his China journey to create. Over the years, the space is no longer a "space between" but rather "a space," in his own words, "filled with dancing sparks ready to ignite new realities—new understandings."[26] May we find our way to that place together—and linger there ten thousand years.

23   Wayne Higby, "Into the Unknown: Imagination and the 'Space Between,'" keynote address
      at the College of Fine Arts at Shanghai University, November 8, 2000.
24   Wayne Higby, "Kong.Flux," keynote address at the International Academy of Ceramics Biannual
      Conference, Xi'an, China, September 10, 2008.
25   Yao Yongkang, personal interview, trans. Huang Chunmao, October 21, 2011.
26   Higby 2000 (see note 23).

50   SKYWELL FALLS, 2009. Earthenware glazed stoneware, steel bracket and cable, suspended ceramic tile. 40 feet × 22 feet × 1½ inches, hangs 3 inches out from the wall. 352 tiles, each 24 × 12 × ⅜ inches. Commission for Miller Center for the Arts, Reading Area Community College, Reading, Pennsylvania. Produced in collaboration with Individuality Art Ceramics, Foshan, China

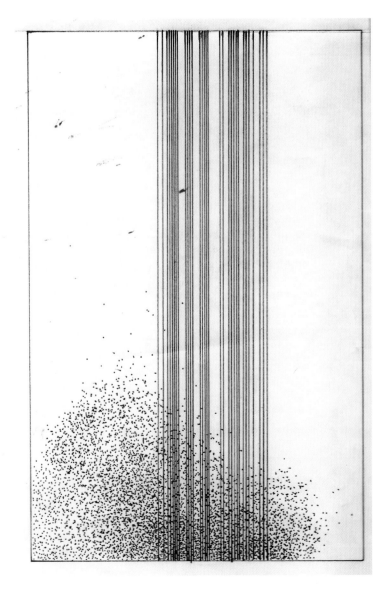

51   Preliminary drawing for SKYWELL FALLS, 2008. Ink on paper. 13 × 9½ inches. Collection of the artist
50   SKYWELL FALLS, 2009 (view from below)

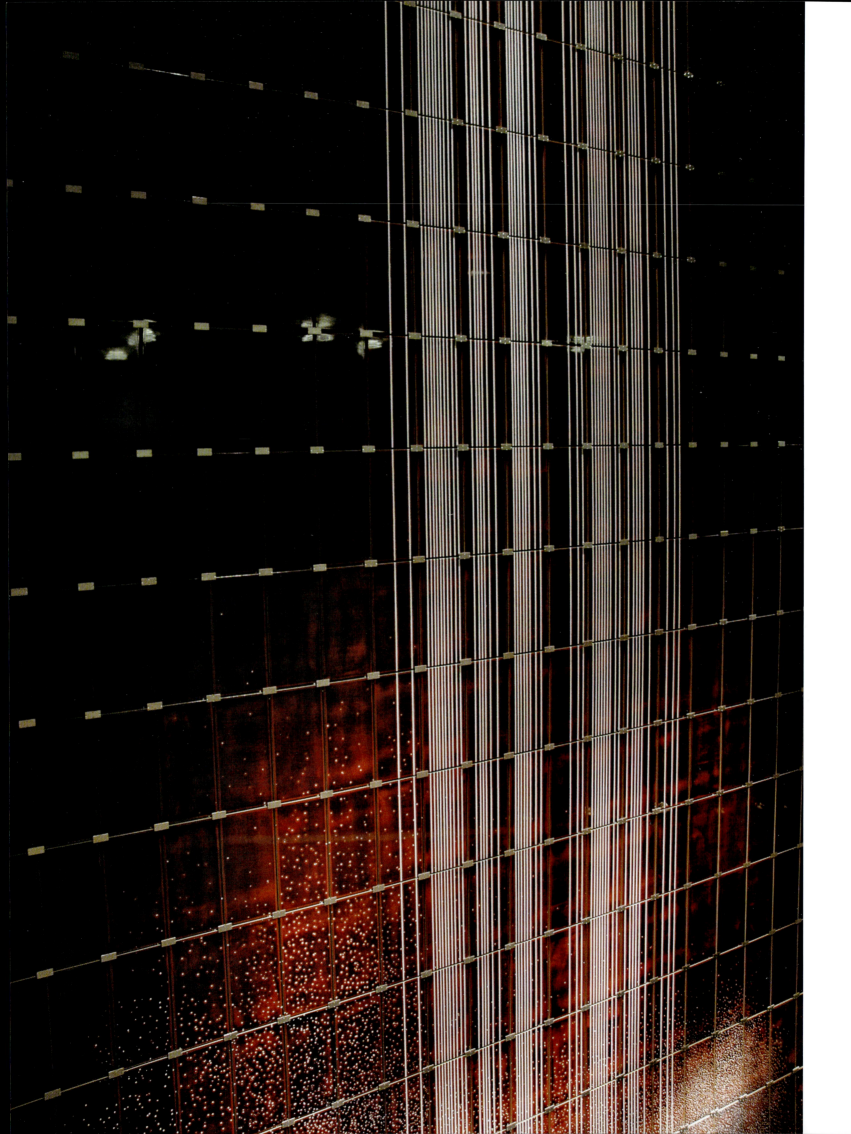

INFINITAS, 2012. Earthenware glazed stoneware. 8 feet × 8 feet × 1½ inches. Collection of the artist

Intangible Notch, SkyWell Falls, and EarthCloud:
The Architectural Reliefs

MARY DRACH MCINNES

A critical facet of Wayne Higby's work that has been central to his recent studio practice and artistic exploration is architectural relief. Since the mid-1990s he has completed three major commissions: *Intangible Notch* (1995) and *Sky-Well Falls* (2009) in Reading, Pennsylvania, and *EarthCloud* (2006/2012) in Alfred, New York. These projects, all commissioned by Alfred University benefactor Marlin Miller, are progressively ambitious in physical scope and conceptual breadth. For almost two decades, Higby has been advancing and elevating a material language and spatial dynamic into an architectural arena. The progress has been cumulative, both linear in nature, with one project informing the next, and cyclical, with the recent installations referencing the artist's earliest themes.

In the three architectural commissions, all developed for buildings designed by the architectural firm Kallmann McKinnell & Wood Architects of Boston, there are two key aspects that have occupied the artist and that are crucial to our experience: a narrative that is grounded in the genre of landscape and the materiality of clay, and an encounter that is structured in the broader architectural space. In the sequence of the projects, these concerns have taken various forms and become more elaborate in scale.

Intangible Notch (1995)

Wayne Higby's initiation into architectural relief was his *Intangible Notch*, constructed for the corporate conference room of Arrow International headquarters (fig. 1, cat. no. 41). The work is roughly square in dimension, measuring eleven feet high by ten feet wide. It is composed of hundreds of tiles, brick-like in size and shape. Formed in wooden press molds, the tiles were cut by hand to generate surface patterning. They were then glazed, raku-fired, and attached to the wall in both horizontal and vertical orientation. At this moment, we see Higby beginning to explore the potential of irregular grids as an organizational structure for repeated form.

Intangible Notch depicts a dramatic landscape. A fiery field of earth tones—rust, auburn, chestnut, sienna, umber—dominates the tile wall. These units coalesce to visually form two jagged rock walls. The title describes a narrow crevice that is revealed by the adjacent rock faces. A vertical band of white sky dominates the notch, running from the top downward to a low horizon. Anchoring the bottom of the notch is a swirling mass of blue water and gray shoreline. The shallow cuts and modest dimensions of the work belie the substantial sense of depth of its illusional landscape.

The narrative topography of *Intangible Notch*—the themes of deep canyons and precipices of the American West—is rooted in the terrain of the artist's life and the landscape of his art. Higby's experiences from his youth in Colorado have been a key inspiration for his thrown and sculpted forms:

1   *Intangible Notch*, 1995.

The introduction of the landscape was a context, a place, and a specific kind of place, the Earth, the land, that sense of my connection to my upbringing in the countryside, riding and looking at the horizon. And then the imaginative, the totally imaginative out-of-body experience that was achievable through illusion that could take you wandering into all kinds of space beyond the physical.[1]

This landscape seen in *Intangible Notch* had emerged fully on his earthenware bowls of the previous two decades. On the raku-fired pots that were his signature work at this time, Higby controlled a firing process known for its unpredictability. He was able to get both the rusty oranges of oxidation as well as the brilliant azures from reduction firing. *Moon Water Bay* (1990, cat. no. 31) is one of the later works in this series. Humble in dimension (twelve by eighteen inches), it is grand in scope. Wheel-thrown and hand-shaped, the bowl's line moves from a narrow base to sides flaring upward and unexpectedly outward into various knobs and emerging boulders. Traversing both the interior and exterior walls of the bowl are fields of pearl as sky and pools of turquoise as water. The bowl's spatial play between interior and exterior landscapes is transferred to the planar surface of *Intangible Notch*.

Intangible Notch is indebted to Higby's vessel production. It replicates the clay body, the firing process, and the narrative imagery of earthenware bowls such as *Moon Water Bay*. These bowls seem to have been flattened, broadened, and extended into the landscape wall. Figuratively, Higby has cut the bowls into tiles, arranged the units, and set them into repose. He has transferred the landscape imagery to a new scale and aesthetic realm. We are, of course, no longer peering at and into a bowl. Instead, we are at a gateway that we visually step into. The scenery of *Intangible Notch* visually draws us into a landscape narrative; simultaneously, its textured surface viscerally pulls us into a material encounter. Ultimately, his architectural reliefs will physically surround us, but at this moment we contemplate an illusion of deep space generated by modest forays away from the flat plane of the wall.

2   *Avatar Beach*, 2002. Earthenware, raku-fired. 8 × 8¼ × 3½ inches. Collection: Burchfield Penney Art Center, Buffalo State College, Buffalo, New York.

While *Intangible Notch* emerged and significantly expanded from his vessel forms, what followed this commission was a surprising compression of scale into a new production of tile sculptures. With a smaller "offspring" of the mural brick, the artist began with a flat, eight-inch square tile. In *Avatar Beach* (2002), for example, he tears out an opening and pushes the clay forward to produce a rocky outcrop (fig. 2). This creates both a positive foreground and a negative opening behind it. The surface is glazed in warm earth tones that are pitted, fractured, and torn. The rugged, sculptural protrusion is countered with a dramatic pictorial field on the left—a black sky with flowing white pools suggestive of water beneath it. As with his bowls, a vast and receding landscape is depicted within the small physical dimensions of these tile sculptures.

Both on the large-scale *Intangible Notch* and the small-scale tile works, Higby's landscape remains literal and resolutely grounded. The metaphorical connections require but one leap of imagination: a torn vertical surface represents a cliff face; a glazed depiction of sky and

1   Part of this essay was taken from my earlier publication on the relief from the Miller Performing Arts Building, see Mary Drach McInnes, "Reflection: EarthCloud," in Wayne Higby, EarthCloud (Stuttgart: Arnoldsche Art Publishers, 2007), p. 33.

water represents sky and water. Abstraction is significant (these are hardly attempts to depict trompe l'oeil landscape), but there tends to be one-to-one correspondences between the image presented and the image imagined. What followed in Higby's next two commissions was the creation of a vocabulary that is more thoroughly abstract and more metaphorically complicated. These projects—*SkyWell Falls* and *EarthCloud*—introduced new avenues of artistic development in material and process, scale and spatial dynamic.

SkyWell Falls (2009)

SkyWell Falls is a large-scale, pictorial installation located at the center of the Miller Performing Arts Center in Reading, Pennsylvania (fig. 3, cat. no. 50). It extends twenty-two feet across, plunges forty feet downward, and hovers three inches over the surface. Typical of most ceramic wall reliefs, this work is made of tile. Unlike other such work, however, including the artist's two other architectural installations, *SkyWell Falls* offers a more two-dimensional vision. Painterly flatness is emphasized over sculptural relief. In viewing the work from afar, our eye sweeps across the glossy surface, unimpeded except by reflections of the sky above and the schematically drawn waterfalls themselves.

SkyWell Falls is a singular work made of multiple parts. It is an immense ceramic tapestry depicting a pearlescent waterfall and is drawn using two elements: point and line. Its channel of ruled lines is narrow and deep, suggesting velocity. In the lower register its kinetic energy springs back upward in a mass of points. These dots suggest the effervescent spray of the falls and seem to gather force. Visually shifting from air to mineral, the points transform into the material that is plucked from the riverbed and carried by the watercourse. The points bump and collide. Sparkling droplets of white glaze cover the bottom edge of *SkyWell Falls*. Viewed closely, the geometry of the points is graphically compromised and vividly more exciting—the points coalesce and merge into each other on the surface. Their cellular structure, while dazzling in surface, is bubbly in texture and ringed in dark, rust-like stains.

Wayne Higby's abstract composition of vertical fall and effervescent drop is set against a crimson background. While the waterfall is central to the design, it is

3 *SkyWell Falls*, 2009.

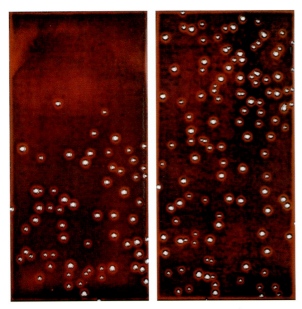

4   *SkyWell Falls*, 2009, tiles.

the red ground of *SkyWell Falls* that dominates the work. The red is rich and deeply shaded at the upper regions and burnished to a bronze-like finish in the middle and lower registers. Together, the bloodstone ground, the speed of the watercourse, and the turbulence of the lower edge create a general sense of wonder and unease. Here brash artifice suggests sublime nature. Higby, using only the basic elements of point, line, and color, provides us with a fantastical realm.[2]

SkyWell Falls is at once materially forged and conceptually fictitious. Its ceramic and glaze physically parallel the stone and glass of its architectural housing and abstractly reference the rock and water of its natural source. Contradictions abound in this installation. While it is a work in clay, *SkyWell Falls* appears metallic—more akin to enamel cloisonné than ceramic tile.[3] This is due to a number of factors. Individually, the tiles are rigorously identical—their one-by-two-foot measurement does not vary. Collectively, the 352 tiles form a grid that is fiercely rectilinear. A narrow black band that frames each tile emphasizes a mathematical precision. The tiles are uniformly thin, their surfaces are flat. These aspects suggest a tensile strength. A series of steel cables and brackets that structurally hold the work in situ reinforce this impression.

An examination of the etched design counters the geometry of the tiles.[4] The imperfectly formed markings on the surface offer an organic reading. For a close analysis, we need to descend a staircase to the ground floor. There we can inspect the true nature of the drawn image. While our initial view of the *Falls* is linear and geometric, the glazes produce a more dynamic impression. The vertical lines seem to be ruler-made but evolve into something more natural in our imaginations. The linear vocabulary gets translated into "water," "stream," "falls." The points, on the other hand, are pools of ivory glaze (fig. 4). Their whiteness is rimmed with red and bronze glazes. These points dissolve into bubbles. The texture is lively: the glaze pools and coagulates on the surface. Positive and negative patterns emerge and diverge into a variety of forms: froth, foam, fizz, bubble, lather, spray, spume, spew, speck. The essential materiality of *SkyWell Falls* is apparent here, and the western New York landscape that inspired the work lies just below its surface.

EarthCloud (2006 and 2012)

In his most ambitious project to date, *EarthCloud*, Higby again projects these same natural elements.[5] But now, the terrain becomes materially more apparent and metaphorically more dramatic and complicated. *EarthCloud* is a two-part, panoramic installation that fills adjacent performing art buildings on the Alfred University campus (fig. 5, cat. no. 53). Some fifteen years passed between the completion of the buildings, and six years passed between the completions of the two parts, but the installation works as a single unit, as if both buildings and art had been conceived and designed together. For more than a decade, the artist worked on *EarthCloud*, and the result is an artistic tour de force in a dramatic building complex that dominates the Alfred University campus and Kanakadea Valley.

EarthCloud is a vast landscape of materiality and metaphor. Here, the artist has drawn on the specific landscape of upstate New York and the broader field of recollection. As we encounter, experience, and reflect upon the work, our foremost impression of *EarthCloud* is its materiality—both in whole and in part (it is composed of over 12,000 porcelain tiles). Its celadon stratigraphy runs along three walls: the lobby wall on the north side of the Miller Performing Arts Center and the south and east walls of the lobby in the Miller Theater at Alfred University. These clay strata—assembled onto metal brackets, stacked into geometric blocks, and stepped across the architectural surface—interact with white wall surfaces and reflect in large glass panes, commanding the attention of visitors to the buildings as well as passersby on the adjacent sidewalks and in the plaza between the buildings.

The scale of *EarthCloud*, perhaps the largest porcelain tile piece ever created, engages us in a manner unlike pedestal sculpture. In both buildings, Higby is acutely aware of the spare modernist architectural vocabulary, the exterior sheathing (large expanses of both brick and glass), and the interior spatial design.[6] *EarthCloud*'s com-

5   *EarthCloud*, 2006.

position in the Miller Performing Arts Center reveals an understanding of these elements in its modular grid, its choice of material, and its unconventional stepped design. Here, the upper panel of *EarthCloud*, with its stacked tiles shifting across the wall, is one of the most startling of Higby's design (fig. 6). A series of horizontal tile bands stretches the length of the north lobby wall. These lines thrust across the space, and while the work's compositional mass covers a majority of the wall, it does not cover the entire surface. Sections of white wall remain and interleave with the composition's frameless tableau. Choosing the dimensions of *EarthCloud* was an intuitive decision by the artist, based on the amount of visual weight the architectural surface could hold.

We experience this work—as we experience *Intangible Notch* and *SkyWell Falls*—as landscape, entering the fiction of the terrain with an imaginative leap. Yet the grand scale of this last work offers us a new experience: we move through it, and it surrounds us. As we stand in front of the work, we project ourselves onto *EarthCloud* as if we are moving through an actual landscape. We project ourselves upon its surface. Susan Stewart, author of *On Longing*, describes this particular type of encounter: "We move through the landscape; it does not move through us. This relation to

2   Part of this essay is taken from my previous writing on this relief. See Mary Drach McInnes, "SkyWell Falls," in Wayne Higby, *SkyWell Falls* (Alfred, N.Y.: Higby, 2011), pp. 3–9.

3   Cloisonné is an ancient technique for decorating metalwork using enamel. It is a process that is used in both the East and the West. The rich color of *SkyWell Falls* is reminiscent of medieval or Renaissance plaques done in champlevé, a kind of enamel work, in which depressions are filled with paste, that is fired and results in a shiny surface. See Hanns Swarzenski and Nancy Netzer, *Catalogue of Medieval Objects: Enamels and Glass* (Boston: Museum of Fine Arts, 1986).

4   *SkyWell Falls* was produced in collaboration with a ceramics factory in Foshan, China. Higby created the design initially in pencil, transferred it to a digital file, and after editing sent it electronically to the factory. See McInnes 2007 (see note 1), pp. 6–8.

5   Mary Drach McInnes 2007 (see note 1), pp. 24–45.

6   Early in the architectural construction, Higby was asked to consider a large-scale project for the new Miller building and the lobby was set aside for a work by him. Wayne Higby, personal interview, April 2007.

6   *EarthCloud*, 2006.

the landscape is expressed most often through an abstract projection of the body upon the natural world."[7] Our experience is reminiscent of the spectator "installed" in Romantic landscape painting, who, in facing Nature, loses himself to the sublime. *EarthCloud*'s shimmering surface and architectural realm encompass us.

A shift in scale—from imposing landscape to intimate tile—unexpectedly marks our participation with the work. We investigate the details of the surface, and its sections evoke a range of associations. *EarthCloud* elicits two extreme and opposing sensations: first, that of being held within something, then that of our holding something. This is the juxtaposition between the gigantic and the miniature. As Stewart expresses it: "Both the miniature and the gigantic may be described through metaphors of containment—the miniature as contained, the gigantic as container."[8] In a handful of tile variations, we read a multitude of meanings.

EarthCloud is composed of six tile variations, each marked by different geometries and depths of relief, and each having required significant labor to produce.[9] Five of these are used in the arts center and a sixth is added in the theater. The most numerous of the tile types is the smooth field tile. These short blocks are faceted, with a raised edge running along the horizontal centerline of the surface. The tile is laid on its side when attached to the wall and oriented horizontally. Even these plain tiles reveal their individuality. Some tiles are blemished with small pits and fissures; all have slight inconsistencies on the surface. Coated with celadon glaze, the tiles show a subtle range of tonalities—willow green, pale turquoise, robin's-egg blue. Color is fused into a highly

7   Susan Stewart, *On Longing: Narratives of the Miniature, the Gigantic, the Souvenir, the Collection* (Durham, N.C.: Duke University Press, 1993), p. 71.

8   Ibid.

9   For the first incarnation of *EarthCloud*, Lee Somers, Higby's studio assistant for this project, cut all the plain field tiles. The artist has calculated that they cut approximately 40,000 pounds of porcelain for this work. Wayne Higby, personal interview, April 2007. For the 2012 addition, Benjamin DeMott and Lee Somers cut all the tiles, under the direction of Wayne Higby. Wayne Higby, personal interview, August 2012.

10   The geology also reflects the area's past industry. The New York State College of Ceramics owes its existence to its ceramic predecessors in Alfred, which included The Celadon Company. The Celadon Company operated at the turn of the century and was located on a site now occupied by Alfred University. It utilized shales from local quarries for the manufacturing of ceramic roof and decorative architectural tiles.

reflective surface, evoking across broad stretches of the wall a patch of sky or watery surface. The glaze is crackled in spots, suggesting the brittleness of ice, and light shimmers on the surface as it does on water or a frozen pool.

Higby and two assistants hand-cut four of the tile types, lending them various meteorological or topographic definitions in progressively higher relief. Twice the length of the field units, these tiles show surfaces that are modeled and carved on a base block of clay similar in shape to the field tiles. The planar surfaces of added or excised shapes tend to be smooth, while the edges and ends of these geometries are ragged or torn (fig. 7). In addition, these relief tiles were sandblasted after glazing, rendering a somewhat softer, less reflective surface.

The second type of tile has triangular, diagonal cuts in low relief falling from the upper right to the lower left. Prism-shaped pieces of clay (the positive correlates of the cut triangular troughs) adhere to many of these tiles. The sandblasting process has highlighted the tiles' sharp points and produced a form that, in the assembled multiples of the installation, suggests wind-blown rain or sleet. The third and fourth tile units are celadon composites with inclusions of rectangular forms oriented to emphasize horizontal layering. The difference between these two tiles is that one has a preponderance of long rectangular slabs, while the other has more cubic additions. Each unit of both types has the visual appearance of sedimentary rock, but the assembled units can be read as either stratified stone or cloud. The fifth tile type is of highest relief. Torn sections of clay are built up at various angles. These tiles were glazed white, fired, and sandblasted to a subtle sheen. Individually, tiles of this type describe chunks of blasted, eroded rock. When assembled they also evoke cumulus clouds, their edges deckled, hovering among darker clouds and sky.

In *EarthCloud* we realize that solid matter itself is a central rhetorical element. Clay is not simply the material used but is the subject projected. Clay is earth—till, strata, outcrop. Higby's porcelain stratigraphy echoes the bedrock that defines the Alfred landscape. *EarthCloud* is directly inspired by the rural countryside of Higby's home territory, and its material, technique, and form are redolent of the region's geography.[10] Rows of tiles mimic the horizontal beds of soft Devonian shale and fine-grained sandstone of the Southwestern Plateau. The deeply cut tiles are reminiscent of the carved valleys in Allegany County, their sandblasted edges indicative of the rugged landforms smoothed and etched by glacial action.

Each building's installation has its own key element, and the Miller Theater brings us an extreme exploration of relief and rock, celadon and cliff. Anchoring the end of the south wall is a grand field that moves across the upper level of the lobby and plummets down along the stairwell. Here, the variations of tile signify, most forcefully, cliff face and waterfall. The vertical fall in rock, which reminds us of the vertical torrent of *SkyWell Falls*, is visually stunning. It physically fills the space and visually flows over the windows that look out across the valley.

Clay is also water—rain, ice, pool. With *EarthCloud* Higby evokes the aquatic and atmospheric realms as well as the terrestrial. Bands of tiles may be read as clouds scuttling across the sky, rain and sleet falling from lower formations, all set against the clear sky evoked by the field tiles. The tiles modeled in relief are cumulus, altocumulus, stratocumulusclouds. And in the Performing Arts Center, Higby fills the lower lobby level at the C. D. Smith Theater entrance to explore this metaphor extensively. Rain streaks down

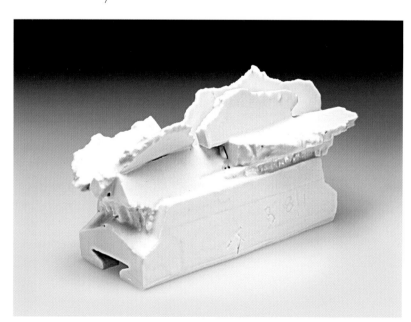

7   *EarthCloud*, 2006, tile 4¼ × 10¼ × 5 inches.

into the lower atmosphere, or alternately, into a watery pool. Again, the artist directly refers to the surrounding environs— to Alfred's dramatic skies, long vistas, and nearby glacial lakes.

To this rich and robust landscape, Higby added a new metallic tile for the recent Miller Theater installation. He announces the drama and spectacle of the theater's productions in 500 brilliant gold field tiles. These units mimic the celadon field tiles in size and shape, but their surfaces are scored horizontally in a rough manner that allows light to flicker on the surface (fig. 8). Embedded into the white and celadon tile assemblies, these gold streaks evoke both mineral veins running through strata and the sun piercing through clouds. Adding an element of excitement, the gold bands extend outward from a prominent corner of the theater lobby in long strands of light. Higby has utilized the theater's visibility— the façade is encased in large floor-to-ceiling glass panels—to create a visual thrill for theatergoers as they approach the entrance. This encounter is particularly effective at night, as one walks into the building, anticipating a theatrical production. The gold is central to *EarthCloud*'s performance, and it acts as a precursor to the interior performance that will follow on the main stage.

The installation is an exploration of metamorphosis. The title, *EarthCloud*, captures this play between the tectonic and atmospheric realms. Ground and sky turn over in the work; rock formations transform into clouds, giving us a tumbling sensation. The physical and the incorporeal are in continuous transition. The sculptural ambiguity of each variant of tile and the largely monochromatic range of color allow for a shifting of associations as we reflect on *EarthCloud*.

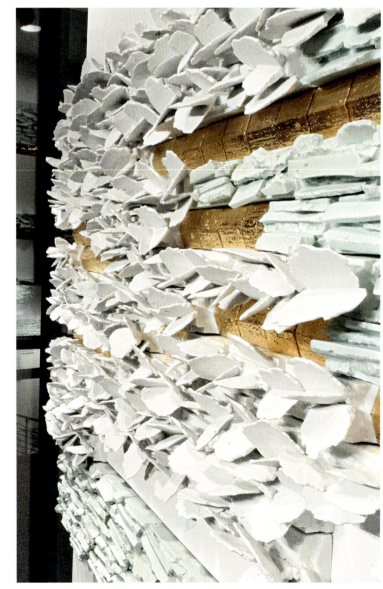

EarthCloud is not cartographic. It does not contain a uniform scale or measurable distances. We read the work across the architectural surface, and there is an oscillation of scale, of association, and of meaning. And viewing *EarthCloud* at night offers us the most layered reading. In the evening the relief's landscape is reflected onto the adjacent windows (fig. 9). Standing in the lobby of either building, we are flanked by the work and its reflection, and beyond the reflection, glimpses of the other building's installation. We look at the work both in and through the window. The doubling of imagery, with the translucent reflection of a near segment layered over our view of another, distant section, is heady. *EarthCloud* is a grand celadon landscape that is spatially and conceptually dynamic.

Higby's physical and imaginative journeys are recorded in his three architectural reliefs. Over a period of nearly two decades he has worked to capture and transform in greater scale, drama, and complexity the realms of rock, sky, and water of his earlier thrown bowls and constructed sculptures. These large, fixed installations are the cumulative expression of the artist's professional life, a studio

8   *EarthCloud*, 2012.

9 *EarthCloud*, 2006/2012.

practice that reveals an early and abiding connection with landscape and a transformation of this connection into a subjective reading of the natural world. Encountering the works, we see over many fields, across material surfaces, and through metaphorical connotations. *Intangible Notch*, *SkyWell Falls*, and *EarthCloud* reflect the whole of Wayne Higby's life in art.

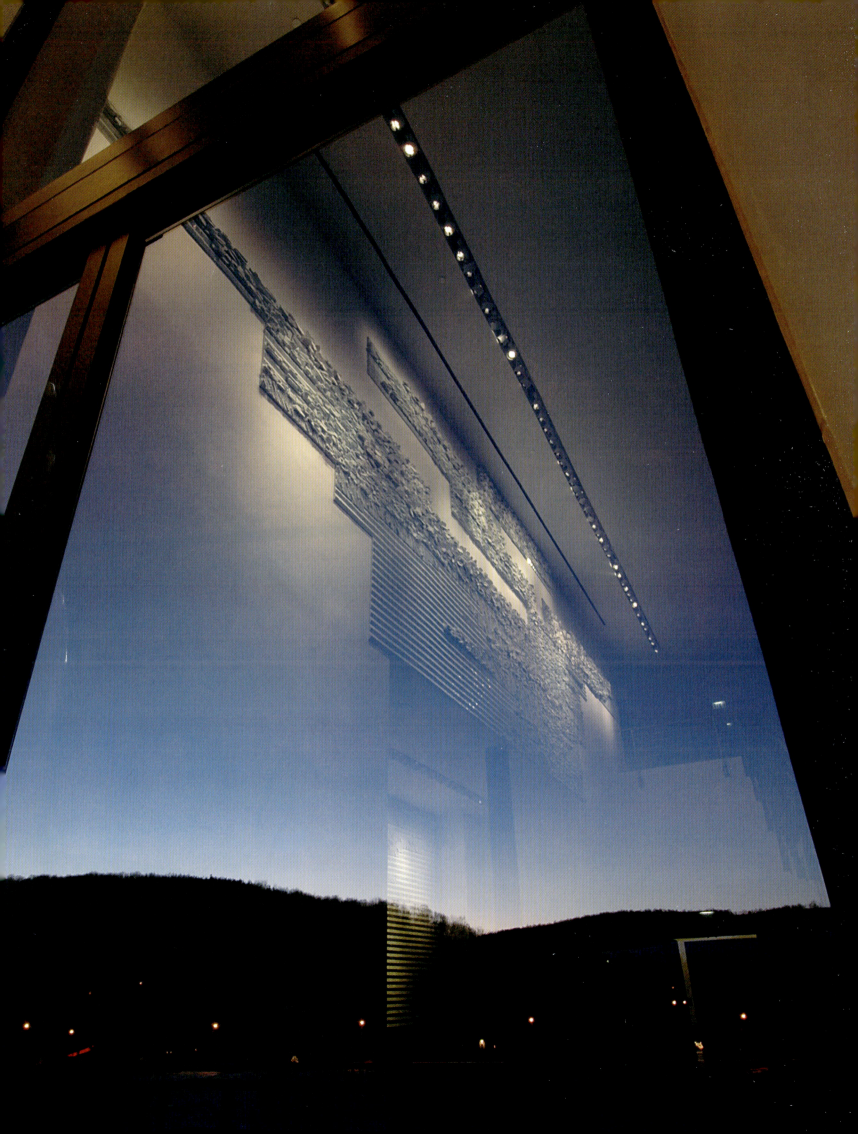

54   CLOUD 1, 2011. Pen, ink on paper. 30 × 22½ inches. Collection of the artist
55   CLOUD 6, 2011. Pen, ink on paper. 30 × 22 inches. Collection of the artist

56   Computer composite of EARTHCLOUD, 2006. Digital print on paper. 35 × 46½ inches. Image produced by Lee Somers and Alex Dericco. Collection of the artist
57   EARTHCLOUD SKETCH / GOLD 3, 2012. Glazed porcelain with gold luster. 15¾ × 27 × 7 inches. Collection of the artist
58   EARTHCLOUD SKETCH / GOLD 1, 2012. Glazed porcelain with gold luster. 12½ × 18½ × 4 inches. Collection of the artist
59   EARTHCLOUD SKETCH / 4, 2012. Glazed porcelain. 15¾ × 27 × 7 inches. Collection of the artist

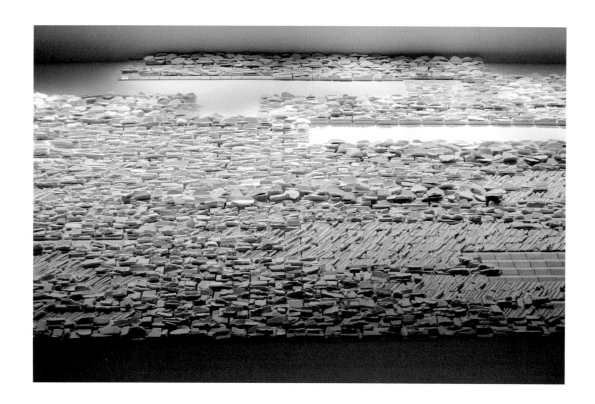

53   EARTHCLOUD, 2006/2012. 12,000 hand-cut, glazed porcelain tiles. Design includes 5,000 square feet connecting two buildings.
      Permanent installation: Miller Performing Arts Complex, commission for Alfred University, Alfred, New York

Reflection

WAYNE HIGBY

Standing looking into a mirror is a common practice. One sees an image of one's self. One sees a projection of a seemingly concrete but illusive truth. Lingering at the mirror, looking deeply, provokes an oddly compelling self-consciousness. What does a reflection reveal? As I stare into the mirror at myself, I wonder where the true self resides in relation to the image. A review of one's life can start there. A life offered in a reflection has some stories to reveal. Is it possible to get behind — on the other side of — or inside the image of things?

This may, in fact, be the central question that has driven my work as an artist. One might ask: "Why have you always worked with imagery?" I might very well answer: "It is a place to start." Emerson wrote: "All the facts of nature are nouns of the intellect, and make the grammar of the eternal language."[1] My artist statement has evolved to read: "Earth, sky, time, light, space: my work is a meditation on the relationship between mind and matter. It is not about landscape."

Making is a form of thinking and knowing. Seeing, making, thinking, and knowing merge into a process of discovery and self-reification that continually guides me as a meaningful means to navigate the sea of ever-drifting doubt. I engage landscape as the panoramic outer membrane of an inner manifestation of unity — a silent, unseen, unknowable resonance of coherence.

For as long as I can remember I have deeply admired the work of those American artists referred to as the luminists. I am partial to Fitz Hugh Lane, John F. Kensett, and Martin Johnson Heade. Barbara Novak writes in her book *American Painting of the Nineteenth Century*: "The luminist looked at nature … with a supernatural eye."[2] This approach suggests a concern for a mental picture rather than an exact rendering of nature. The luminist landscape is a form of conceptual art and in that sense echoes the Chinese painters' idea of spirit resonance, which acknowledges landscape painting as a mindscape rather than an exercise in form likeness. Over time, I have learned, through my own intuitive conviction, that I share a kindred artistic intention with intrinsically situated aspects of American and Chinese philosophy.

Admittedly, from time to time, my particular interest in American landscape has seemed to a degree anachronistic within the curatorial framework of contemporary art. Nevertheless, I have stubbornly adhered to the convictions of my own artistic doubt. Such convictions have included an interest in craft and the ingenuity of the hand. Craft is also the art of paying attention: an ethic of observation and of making with intention, skill, and care. Yes, making is thinking and a way of knowing.

As an adolescent, my world was paint, paper, sticks, and clay. We communicated. As a result, I was given the gift of self-realization. I developed a deep respect for earthborn materials as a context for revealed truth. Throughout my childhood I remained encapsulated within a cocooning sense of otherness. I was held within the shell of my emotions — my own seemingly isolated world of mind and matter. I grew up alone: no brothers, no sisters. There was silence and space for imagination. My first memory is of bright sunlight and the sparkling, pink granite dust of the Colorado mountains as well as the clean, fresh smell of the air after the rain. Longing has always possessed me. Longing for what? I have never been sure: a connection, contact, knowledge, and sense of place, revelation. My sensual connection with the world drives wonder. Longing has been tempered by making. I have descended into myself through a contact with sensual materials. I have courted meaning.

The horizon line always beckons. I have introduced it repeatedly into the work. What is out there, where the sky meets the sea? Perhaps one can slip through that razor's edge of line and float free in a world of all-embracing awareness. The repetition of line and its rhythmical attention to evolving pattern has formed the basis of structure in the mental and visual orientation of my work. Patterned sequences repeatedly suggest a mental picture, an ideal rather than a realistic rendering of image. I have always been assisted by process: by the nature of material and its teaching. I have continually tried to be vulnerable to material and process, merging my conceptual ideal with found coordinates that assist navigation to a point of arrival. I began as a painter.

1   Ralph Waldo Emerson, *The Basic Writing of an American Sage*, ed. Edward C. Lindeman
     (New York: New American Library, Mentor Books, 1947), p. 114.
2   Barbara Novak, *American Painting of the Nineteenth Century: Realism, Idealism and the American
     Experience* (Oxford and New York: Oxford University Press, Inc., 1980), p. 76.

As an undergraduate student in the art school at the University of Colorado, I thought that I would be a painter, but I had significant doubt. I did not fall easily into the conceits of the 1960s' art establishment. I did not understand "art." I was lost, but excited about what I might eventually discover. I kept working. My teacher told me that my paintings were beautiful. It was clear that was not enough. He couldn't seem to help.

In 1963, I left school to take a trip around the world with close friends of my family. As might be expected, my entire life was changed as a result. In India I had a shattering confrontation with my naïve, egocentric sureness of being. I had never before witnessed such pounding rhythms of survival. Later, I discovered Minoan pottery in the Heraklion Museum on Crete. It still informs the basis of my personal point of view and passion for ceramic art. Returning to school, I was determined to make my life count: to take charge of my opportunities whatever they might be. I began to develop a philosophical position, a personal belief system to live by.

I found some individuals who seemed to be following an ideal I could identify with, or, perhaps more truthfully, they found me. They reached out to witness and to nurture my desire. I met Betty Woodman, who was a studio potter at the time. I took classes with her in the evenings at the "Fire House," which was a converted fire station managed by the City of Boulder Parks and Recreation Department. Betty introduced me to Paul Soldner, and I studied briefly with Jim and Nan McKinnell when Jim was invited to teach ceramics at the university. I also studied with Manuel Neri, who was the first to show me the work of Peter Voulkos, John Mason, and Henry Takemoto. Their art was a revelation. In particular, Takemoto's work spoke to me. I was inspired, energized, and committed to follow these artist mentors. I responded purely visually. I did not comprehend what was going on, but I could feel the energy, a visceral connection to a new world of possibility. There was a sense of the hand and of the intellect, of emotional power and confrontation with tradition. There was something called "craft" and something called "art." There were rumored indications of a burgeoning new community of makers across the country. There was something called the American craft movement: concepts, genealogies, shamans, and followers. These artists made things with their skilled hands via processes that transformed materials of the earth into poetic, sympathetic objects. There was a sense of living humanity at stake: an investment in others and the ethics of community. I wanted to belong. I wanted to stand for something. I wanted to be recognized by those I admired. I felt deeply that I had something to say. *Objects: USA*, which opened in 1969, was the first major exhibition to track this new era. I was included as one of the youngest artists represented.

The first exhibit of my ceramic work took place in 1965 before I graduated from undergraduate school: *Betty Woodman, Maria Martinez, Wayne Higby*. I had no idea what it meant at the time. Of course, nobody knew. Betty was far from being a nationally recognized artist. She was a local potter. Maria was contained in a narrow scholarly appreciation for the American Indian, and I was a precocious, inexperienced young male wannabe. Almost fifty years has passed since then. The journey from a time that I think of as enchanted and far away may now look ordained, but that is how history works; nothing is inevitable until it seems so by the arrival. Individuals make a difference. Individual meetings, friend-

1   Wayne Higby and *EarthCloud* 2006/2012.

ships, rivalries, and dreams do change the world. A small raku box of mine was juried into the national exhibition *Craftsmen USA '66*. It was shown at the American Craft Museum in New York. I went to graduate school at the University of Michigan to study ceramics with Fred Bauer and John Stephenson.

I married my high-school sweetheart, Donna Claire Bennett, in a small village near Paris, France, in 1966, just before I began my MFA studies at the University of Michigan. She became the foundation of my life and eventually my career. My son, Austin Myles, and daughter, Sarah Lark, soon arrived to fuel my commitment to work. Donna became my chief critic. Her untimely death from cancer in 2004 nearly ended my will to continue in the studio. I hung her picture over my workbench and dug in. My memory of her has firmly and gently encouraged me into the present. I see her in my reflection, in my effort to recall the past, to ponder the image in the mirror.

I began my teaching career in the Midwest at the University of Nebraska at Omaha in 1968. It was a good place to start, and I immediately went to work making the pieces for my first one-person exhibition, which was held at Omaha's Joslyn Art Museum in December 1968. We left Omaha in 1970 for a teaching job at the Rhode Island School of Design. While working there, I received an invitation from Paul Smith, the director of the American Craft Museum in New York, to mount a one-person show at the museum in the spring of 1973. Then the call came from Alfred University. That fall I began my current thirty-nine years with the School of Art and Design, Division of Ceramic Art, Alfred University.

At some point along the way, I discovered that I was born on a Wednesday, squarely in the middle of the workweek. Perhaps that explains it: the artist-professor bifurcation. I live as the hyphen, as the bridge between the two, inviting others back and forth across the space between. All artists are teachers, of course. It takes a certain hardened patience, however, to put up with academia. It is the students. They are a force field of irresistible life and energy. I work at Alfred, and I continually meet highly gifted students. In the fall of each year I am born again into the creative life of other individuals. They inspire me. They challenge me. There is vitality in the energy exchange that is deeply genuine, sometimes overwhelmingly powerful. My teaching mantra is "I am here to help you discover what you already know—to build on that awareness, discipline it, and use it to explore the unknown." I think of myself as an audience. I just want to be the best audience possible. Teaching art is to be an informed, sensitive witness and to cross that threshold to engage, challenge, and encourage. The process shines light into my life and strengthens my commitment to the studio: my studio—my art, which lies at the center of all that I am.

I have just completed a piece I call *EarthCloud* (fig. 1). It will very likely remain the major and perhaps defining work of my career. It has been eleven years in process. *EarthCloud* encompasses over 5,000 square feet and joins the interior space of two buildings that face each other across an open plaza. *EarthCloud* is made of approximately 12,000 hand-cut porcelain tiles. This work brings all my thoughts and feelings about my work, since my earliest beginnings as an artist, into the force field of an extraordinary reality.

One of the significant aesthetic conditions of *EarthCloud* involves the dynamics of reflection. The factual material elements are embedded in the architecture but also in an unfathomable reveal associated with multiple-layered reflections in the glass that serves as the external façade of the buildings. The reality of architectural space is transformed into an infinity of illusory dimension—a mindscape. I am reminded of this as I stand staring at myself in the mirror. The image of self is restless. It seems to expand and contract as it intersects fleeting moments of cognition.

Acknowledgments

Philadelphia April 2, 2010: I was in town for the National Council on Education for the Ceramic Arts NCECA ceramics conference. Helen W. Drutt English had left a message on my cell phone—come to lunch tomorrow as I'm visiting with Peter Held. I knew who Peter was. Well, I knew him just about enough to say hello. As curator of the nationally recognized Ceramics Research Center at Arizona State University Art Museum he had put some wonderful exhibitions together, most recently the Karen Karnes retrospective. I went to lunch. Peter was gracious and Helen was fun, bright and brilliant as always. As I left Peter said "Send me some images."

Now, I have them both to thank for envisioning my retrospective and this book that accompanies it. Helen illuminates possibility. Peter Held listens carefully and works with consistency and patience to make ideas become concrete realities. I am greatly indebted to them both. Helen has been the single most important advocate of my art since I began working with her when she opened her gallery in Philadelphia in 1974. Peter has brought all those years into focus and insightfully revealed the intellectual and aesthetic continuity of my life's work.

I must also thank everyone who has helped over the years to mentor and inspire my life and art. My wife, Donna, was at the center of most of it. Without her I would not have had a career. Family is critical and mine has been a genuinely loving, supportive influence—patient and tolerant of my eccentricities. It is fun to have an artist around. Well, maybe not always.

Recently, as the result of being honored in 2005 with the Robert C. Turner Chair at Alfred University and its development fund, I have been able to hire an assistant. The individuals involved have been amazing, inspiring my work and my life with revitalizing spirit. Their commitment to helping me see projects through has been extraordinary. They are pure magic—thank you Lee Somers, Ian McMahon, Benjamin DeMott. Currently, Mahlon Huston is my right hand and without him this retrospective project would not have come to fruition. He is a master craftsman and artist. He certainly helped immeasurably in putting the show on the road.

I would also like to acknowledge all the gifted students I have had the opportunity to work with. They have taught me to see beyond my own small world. Thank you to my colleagues across the campus at Alfred University who have been a source of support for my art and teaching career. My close, long-time, colleagues in the Division of Ceramic Art— Anne Currier, John and Andrea Gill, Walter McConnell and Linda Sikora have greatly inspired and informed my art and teaching with their dynamic engagement of our collaborative efforts. I treasure our friendship.

Dirk Allgaier who heads up ARNOLDSCHE Art Publishers deserves a gold medal of acknowledgment and thanks for his commitment to making the beautiful book that accompanies the retrospective. Dirk is a young visionary. His unique insight, intelligence and charm are compelling attributes that inspire and guide the publication of rare, elegant, and sophisticated books on art that are, in fact, art in and of themselves. I felt very privileged to work with Karina Moschke, Dirk's colleague and extraordinary designer. Her sensitivity to my work and her wonderful gift for design are a revelation. Additionally, Arnoldsche's project manager Wiebke Ullmann gave me great confidence throughout the process. It is actually impossible to overstate how importantly true, skilled professionalism counts. I am very grateful to have had such a marvelous publishing team to work with.

Henry Sayre, Tanya Harrod, Ezra Shales, Mary McInness and Carla Coch are all significant scholars who graciously responded to the request for material. I feel that, as a result of their contributions, the exhibition catalogue gets in and under the artwork to provide real scholarship that investigates the nature of ideas and, therefore, makes the retrospective document a significant contribution to the field over and beyond the typical celebration of the artist. This appeals to me greatly and highlights my own commitment to writing and teaching.

There are so many individuals behind the scenes of a retrospective endeavor. I want to acknowledge them and thank them all. Linda White has for many years been a significant help to my career, and for the retrospective she organized, collated, and recorded the vast amount of information in my files from the early 1970s to the present. This enormous job she did with skill and humor. Both are very much appreciated. My thanks go to the staff of the Arizona State University Art Museum and its Ceramics Research Center as well as everyone at each of the exhibition venues. And to the photographers, especially my long-time friend the amazing Brian Oglesbee and to John Copland as well as to members of the *EarthCloud* team—without excellent photos it would be as if the work did not exist.

A singular acknowledgment is due for the help and emotional support I have received from my close friend Lisa. Dr. Lisa Lantz and I share a professional commitment to our art forms and a tough realistic and romantic understanding of what it really takes to be an artist.

Finally, I wish to acknowledge, with a very special thank you, the Windgate Charitable Foundation for its extraordinary support. The Foundation is significantly transforming opportunity and scholarship in the visual arts. Thank you also to the Friends of Contemporary Ceramics.

Here at the conclusion of these remarks, I want to acknowledge Marlin and Ginger Miller, who have inspired my life and work in such an enormous way that I am now far beyond having the words to articulate my feelings of deep gratitude. Their generosity and commitment to my work has truly changed my life and career in ways I could never have dreamed possible.

One morning in Philadelphia particles began to align, and, like iron filings drawn to a magnetic field, the myriad of elements that make a retrospective project came together. The opportunity to relive my history as an artist is humbling and infused with feelings of pain and pleasure all of which allow me to catch a glimpse of meaning. Thank you to all the generous individual and institutional collectors of my work who acquired it and have now allowed it to reenter the exhibition world. Without them there would be no career to review. The artworks as a whole as well as the memories imbedded in each piece are potent reminders of the struggle, the doubt, and the excitement involved in being an artist.

2   Wayne Higby working on *EarthCloud*, artist's studio. Alfred Station, New York, 2011.

Chronology

1943

Donald Wayne Higby is born on May 12 in Colorado Springs, Colorado. His father, Donald Wayne Higby Sr., is a lawyer who worked at one time as the district attorney in Colorado Springs. His mother, Mary Elizabeth Bates (Betty Higby), is a community activist who eventually became superintendent of the U.S. Mint in Denver, Colorado.

1948–60

Resides during childhood in the Austin Bluffs area of Palmer Park, east of Colorado Springs, which provides a vantage point to the majestic Pikes Peak.
As an only child, he relies on the company of his horses and rides exploring the canyons and mesas of his Austin Bluffs home (figs. 1, 2). He also rides competitively.
Re-edited excerpt from an autobiographical essay: "A Search for Form and Place," *Ceramics Monthly* 37/10 (1989).
Civil War general and railroad tycoon William Jackson Palmer turned a cliff-mesa wilderness east of Colorado Springs into a recreational area and named it Palmer Park. He established a look-out point high on a mesa's rim. Looking west he could see the city of Colorado Springs. Then looking north and slowly moving his eyes southward, the general could also take in a panoramic view of the Front Range of the Rocky Mountains, including Pikes Peak and the majestic rocks of the Garden of the Gods. Concentrating his view south, he could catch a glimpse of the Sangre de Cristo Mountains of New Mexico. I grew up at Grand View Point. That is to say, I lived in a house built directly below the Point (fig. 3).
Receives several scholarships in elementary school, which provide an opportunity to study at the Colorado Springs Fine Arts Center.

1961

Begins his undergraduate studies at the University of Colorado Boulder, Colorado, majoring in pre-law to follow in the footsteps of his father. After experiencing the paucity of illustrations in law books, he switches his major to art.
An early inspiration is his maternal grandfather, Roy Bates, a carpenter and an artisan who lived and worked in Kansas City, Kansas.

1963–64

Takes a leave from undergraduate work to travel around the world with family friends. A formative experience while in Calcutta, India, sees abject poverty firsthand; he starts to ask serious questions of himself and begins to think about teaching as a profession. "I began to see it as a means to celebrate opportunity and accept responsibility." Visits the Heraklion Museum, Crete, December 4, 1963. Viewing Minoan pottery changes his life and aesthetic (fig. 4). "On that day I became a potter."

2

1

3

1964

Returns to the university and continues his studies with the painter George Woodman who introduces Higby to his wife, potter Betty Woodman. Enrolls in university pottery class. Its physical distance from mainstream art activities has implications of psychological freedom. Enrolls in a summer-school course with sculptor Manuel Neri, who introduces him to the work of Peter Voulkos, John Mason, and Henry Takemoto. Excerpt from "Reflection," autobiographical document, 1/2012:

I also studied with Manuel Neri, who was the first to show me the work of Peter Voulkos, John Mason, and Henry Takemoto. Their art was a revelation. In particular, Takemoto's work spoke to me. I was inspired, energized, and committed to follow these artist mentors. I responded purely visually. I did not comprehend what was going on, but I could feel the energy, a visceral connection to a new world of possibility. There was a sense of the hand and of the intellect, of emotional power and confrontation with tradition.

1965

During last year at the university, gets involved with an additional pottery class at the "Fire House," where Betty Woodman teaches for the Boulder Parks and Recreation Department. Meets Paul Soldner, who demonstrates the Japanese raku process to students. Studies with Jim and Nan McKinnell in a summer session.
Father dies of cancer.
First exhibition of work at the University of Colorado Boulder Art Gallery, with Betty Woodman and Maria Martinez.

1966

Continues to think about Minoan and Islamic pottery. Receives BFA from the University of Colorado Boulder, major in art education, minor in painting and ceramics. Marries childhood sweetheart, Donna Claire Bennett in Marnes-la-Coquette, France; she also has a BFA from the University of Colorado Boulder (figs. 5, 6).
Honeymoons in southern Europe, including several weeks in Florence, Italy, with George and Betty Woodman.
Begins graduate studies at the University of Michigan, Ann Arbor; meets Fred Bauer, Patti Warashina, John Stephenson, Susanne Stephenson, and John Glick (fig. 7).
Son, Austin Myles, is born September 6.
His first year of graduate school is significantly influenced by his relationship with his teacher Fred Bauer and his wife Patti (now Warashina). Meets collector Bob Pfannebecker when he visits the Bauers' studio. Receives a prize for his raku box in the exhibition *Craftsmen USA '66* exhibited at the Museum of Contemporary Crafts, New York. Photographs of the piece are published in *Craft Horizons* magazine.

1967

Develops a close association with his professor John Stephenson.
Artist Richard DeVore selects his work for *Sixteen Michigan Ceramists*, Cranbrook Academy of Art, Michigan.

4

5+6

1968

Completes MFA with a major in ceramics and minor in serigraphy. Daughter, Sarah Lark, is born May 13.

Begins teaching at University of Nebraska, Omaha.

S. C. Johnson Company acquires Egyptian paste and earthenware *Storage Jar* for the seminal exhibition *Objects: USA*. His pottery is non-functional with an emphasis on the interdependence of surface and form. Excerpt from statement for the *Objects: USA* catalogue: Specifically, in relation to pottery, I am impressed and influenced by the past. I use the past as a catalogue of ideas which inspires me to create objects in clay that express my concern with visual beauty rather than function.

Has first major one-person exhibition at Joslyn Art Museum, Omaha, Nebraska (fig. 8).

1969

Travels throughout the Southwest, West Coast, and the plains states of Montana, Colorado, and Nebraska. "I rediscovered landscape."

Invited to participate in the *Young Americans 1969* exhibition held at the Museum of Contemporary Crafts. His *Raku Storage Jar* is the first time he incorporates the use of landscape imagery.

Is a visiting, summer-school lecturer in ceramics at the University of Washington, Seattle. Lives in Howard Kottler's home while teaching. Executes his first raku landscape box.

Objects: USA travels to the National Collection of Fine Arts, Smithsonian Institution, Washington, D.C., continuing throughout Europe and the Middle East.

Meets artists Ken Ferguson, Howard Kottler, and Jerry Rothman at the annual National Council on Education for the Ceramic Arts (NCECA), Kansas City, Missouri. All three become important mentors.

1970

Major changes begin to occur in Higby's work as a result of his summer travels as his observations of the landscape dominate the dialogue between form and surface.

Receives a summer residency grant from resident director David Shaner at the Archie Bray Foundation in Helena, Montana. Has a solo exhibition at the conclusion of his residency.

Meets Robert Turner and Peter Voulkos at the NCECA conference held in San Francisco, California. Turner is responsible for inspiring Higby to join the Alfred University faculty in 1973.

Exhibition with Sherri Smith at the Colorado Springs Fine Arts Center Museum. Sherri Smith is an important childhood friend who later becomes a renowned fiber artist.

Appointed assistant professor at Rhode Island School of Design, Providence. Meets Norm Schulman and Dale Chihuly, who are both on faculty.

Meets John Gill, a student at Cornish School of Art, Seattle, Washington. Later John becomes an MFA student at Alfred and then an important friend and colleague at Alfred University.

1971

Visits Val Cushing on a trip to Alfred University, New York, with Norm Schulman.

Richard DeVore extends the first of several invitations to lecture at Cranbrook Academy of Art.

One-person exhibition at Benson Gallery, Bridgehampton, Long Island, New York. Scripps Invitational Ceramics Exhibition at Scripps College, Claremont, California.

Paul Smith, director of the Museum of Contemporary Crafts, takes an interest in the work and eventually becomes a lifelong friend.

7

8

1972

International Ceramics, invitational exhibition, Victoria and Albert Museum, London.

Meets Andrea Gill by chance one day while teaching at the Rhode Island School of Design. She had come to the school on a brief visit. Later Andrea becomes an MFA student at Alfred and then an important friend and colleague at Alfred University.

Assisted by his student Janna Longacre, he creates first site-specific architectural tile installation for the Ceramic Department exhibition, Woods-Gerry Mansion Gallery, Rhode Island School of Design. Egyptian paste with inlaid pattern is used for the tile (fig. 9) This is the first and perhaps only time the medium of Egyptian paste has been used on such a large scale.

1973

One-person exhibition at the Museum of Contemporary Crafts (fig. 10). Potter David Shaner writes catalogue statement:

Once in a great while, an artist's work speaks to us in clear terms— unnecessary to codify or verbalize. Wayne Higby has distinguished himself in this way … As an image-maker Wayne understands and lives close contact with the symbols he chooses to express—a fusion of Man–the Land–and the Spirit.

Teaches summer session at Scripps College. Lives in Paul Soldner's home while teaching.

Appointed associate professor at New York State College of Ceramics, Alfred University. Faculty members at the time include Ted Randall, Robert Turner, and Val Cushing. Purchases 1823 farmhouse, including fifty acres, and builds a studio. Brings horses from Colorado (figs. 11, 12, 13). Receives a National Endowment for the Arts Fellowship grant.

1974

Begins professional gallery associations with Alice Westphal, owner of Exhibit A, Evanston, Illinois, and Helen W. Drutt English of the Helen Drutt Gallery, Philadelphia, Pennsylvania. Participates in *Inaugural Exhibition* at Drutt's gallery.

Helen W. Drutt English becomes an important friend, advisor, and advocate for Higby's work as an artist.

His *White Canyon* landscape container is included in *In Praise of Hands, First World Crafts Exhibition*, Ontario Science Centre, Toronto, Ontario, Canada.

Holds his first solo show for the Exhibit A gallery.

Moves from the slab-constructed boxes to the bowl form. Decides that a less rigid thrown form is more appropriate to the landscape at Alfred, where the hills roll into each other bathed in diffused light.

Meets Don Kaake. Don eventually becomes a friend and indispensible collaborator as technical assistant to numerous art projects.

1976

Holds his first solo show for the Helen Drutt Gallery. His bowl, *Big Basin Pass*, 1976, enters the permanent collection of the Philadelphia Museum of Art, Pennsylvania.

Participates and lectures in conjunction with *American Crafts '76: An Aesthetic View* at the Museum of Contemporary Art, Chicago, Illinois. Excerpt from lecture: "Outline for Ceramics":

To suggest that on careful consideration Oldenburg's soft sculpture is really craft because of his use of traditional craft techniques in their construction or to say that Christo's Valley Curtain should really be included in this exhibition because it uses fiber is obviously overlooking ideas and intentions. Likewise to designate an abstract or super-real piece of sculpture made of metal, wood, clay, or fiber as fine craft simply on the basis of skill, materials, and processes is irrational.

Pottery, not sculpture in clay, is the clearest case in which craft has been transformed into art while at the same time retaining a physical, emotional and psychological essence in the craft tradition.

9

10

1977

Receives his second National Endowment for the Arts Fellowship grant.
Receives Crafts in the Parks grant from the National Park Service. Travels to the Florida Everglades to develop work.
Meets Anne Currier in Boulder, Colorado, while a visiting artist at the University of Colorado Boulder. She later becomes an important friend and colleague at Alfred University.

1978

Elected chairman for the Visual Arts panel, New York State Council on the Arts.
Teaches first summer session at Haystack Mountain School of Crafts in Maine where the surrounding landscape becomes a major theme in his work.
Has his second solo exhibition at Exhibit A gallery.
Ceramic Vessel as Metaphor, Evanston Art Center, Evanston, Illinois, organized by Alice Westphal. Bowl *South Park*, 1977, is included in *Craft: Art and Religion*, Vatican Museum, Rome, Italy.
Along with Joyce Moty and Dale Chihuly is a juror for *Young Americans 1978*. Several Alfred alumni receive top awards.

11

1979

Work is included in the exhibition *A Century of Ceramics in the United States 1878–1978: From Pottery to Painting in Clay*, organized by Garth Clark and Margie Hughto, opens at the Everson Museum of Art, Syracuse, New York. Is a panelist considering the vessel with Betty Woodman, Richard DeVore, and Garth Clark, Syracuse Ceramic Symposium, Syracuse University, New York. Contributes the following poem of A. A. Milne:

Halfway down the stairs is the stair where I sit.
There isn't any other stair quite like it.
I'm not at the bottom,
I'm not at the top; so this is the stair where I always stop.
Halfway up the stairs isn't up and it isn't down.
It isn't in the nursery,
It isn't in the town.
And all sorts of funny thoughts run round in my head.
It isn't really anywhere! It's somewhere else instead!

One-person exhibitions held at the Helen Drutt Gallery and Okun-Thomas Gallery, Saint Louis, Missouri.

1980

Winter Inlet, 1975, a four-part land-scape box-sculpture with lids, is selected for the permanent collection of the Metropolitan Museum of Art, New York (fig. 15). *Winter Inlet* is the first post-WWII ceramic art object to enter the collection.
Elected to the board of directors, Gallery Association of New York State.
Participates in the *8th Chunichi International Exhibition of Ceramic Arts*, Nagoya, Japan.
Takes a sabbatical leave from Alfred University.
Writes and delivers lecture, in conjunction with *A Century of Ceramics in the United States 1878–1978*. *From Pottery to Painting in Clay*, which is frequently referred to as the "Eight Categories Lecture," Toledo Museum of Art, Ohio; Portland Museum of Art, Oregon; and Detroit Institute of Art and International Academy of Ceramics (IAC) conference at New York University. The categories are Functional, Decorative, Vessel, Object, 3-D Drawing, Modern Painting, Modern Sculpture, and Architecture.

12

13

1982

Delivers lecture "The Vessel: Overcoming the Tyranny of Modern Art," NCECA conference, San Jose, California. Excerpt from the presentation, *NCECA Journal* 3/1, was republished in *Choosing Craft: The Artist's Viewpoint*, University of North Carolina Press, 2009.
The vessel is a manifestation of unity in art. It incorporates the complex dynamics of surface and form, seeing and touching, contemplation and use. It is not pure in the modernist sense. It is not a part. It is the sum of the parts. The vessel represents the unity inherent in human experience. "Represents" is a key word, for the art of the vessel is an art of passage. The vessel makes it possible for humanity's past and present to touch in the creation of a form, which marks a path into the future.
Writes the introduction for Philip Rawson's seminal text *Ceramics*, at the invitation of Maurice English, republished by University of Pennsylvania Press in 1984.
A solo exhibition featuring a group of landscape bowls is presented at the Helen Drutt Gallery.
For eleven years the artist turns choreographer for the annual Alfred-Almond high-school musical, beginning with Rodgers and Hammerstein's *The King and I*.

1983

Appointed chair, Division of Ceramic Art, when departments are restructured at Alfred University. Elected to the board of trustees at Haystack Mountain School of Crafts. Becomes a member of the International Academy of Ceramics, based in Geneva, Switzerland. Has work included in the important exhibition *Ceramic Echoes: Historical References in Contemporary Ceramics*, Nelson-Atkins Museum of Art, Kansas City, Missouri, organized by Garth Clark.

1984

Builds an addition to his Alfred Station studio in order to expand firing facilities.
Works in the Omaha brick factory with Betty Woodman and Jun Kaneko and produces an extensive wall structure from old factory bricks (fig. 14). The experience inspires the artist to develop concepts on working in large scale referencing the integration of surface, form, and structural considerations.

1985

Receives New York Foundation for the Arts Fellowship.
Keynote speaker: *Colloquium for the Future*, Haystack Mountain School of Crafts. Excerpt from presentation entitled "Craft as Attitude":
In recognizing craft as attitude we can begin to see that all good works of art share the same reality. Such things as vulnerability and critical evaluation are the tools, which help all artists to move beyond mere expressions of self-indulgence. But the artist must do more than just use these tools skillfully. He or she must disclose the mysteries behind appearances and assumptions. To behold and understand is supremely gratifying. To interpret and reveal is Art. The rest is politics.
Higby is the featured speaker at the NCECA, St. Louis, Missouri. The topic is "Gathering Vision."
Also delivers lecture at the Honolulu Academy of Art, Hawaii.
Writes an article for *Studio Potter* magazine titled "Drawing as Intelligence." Excerpt from the article:
The bowl is me personified. The landscape image is my sense of place and the drawing or line that connects it all is my curiosity seeking to comprehend relationships, searching out thoughts and feelings, unifying surface and form, and trying to uncover meaning. As a visual person I depend on drawing as a way of knowing. I draw to learn and understand.

14

15

1986

Receives the George A. and Eliza Gardner Howard Foundation Fellowship, administered by Brown University, Providence, Rhode Island.

Takes a sabbatical leave from Alfred University for the academic year to develop work in the studio.

Proposes creation of Randall Session for NCECA in honor of its founding father Theodore Randall.

Juror for the Visual Arts Fellowship/ Crafts panel, National Endowment for the Arts.

Delivers lecture "Denying Function" at the *Architecture of the Vessel* symposium, Rochester Institute of Technology, New York. Excerpt from the published text *Ceramics Monthly* 34/6 (1986):

Constantin Brancusi made four large wooden cups between 1917 and 1920. None of these cups were hollow. Therefore, they were definitely not vessels although they carried the image of the pot. Brancusi denied functionality and proclaimed the cup to be an object of pure contemplation. A few ceramic artists in this century have matched what Brancusi did for the cup but with the important difference of retaining the principal formal criteria of hollowness. Thus, rather than turning pottery into sculpture via image, these artists have asked us to reevaluate and contemplate the pot via its essential reality. They have made it clear that function is an undeniable possibility of the vessel and yet they have removed function as a logical conclusion in experiencing the work. These artists have established the definitive limits of the contemporary pot and have given the term "vessel" new meaning.

Work is included in the groundbreaking exhibition *Craft Today: Poetry of the Physical*, American Craft Museum, New York and organized by its director Paul Smith.

Interviewed by Dr. Richard Polsky for the Oral History Collection Project, Columbia University, New York.

Elected vice president of the board of trustees, Haystack Mountain School of Crafts.

1987

Meets businessman, art collector, and Alfred University benefactor Marlin Miller, who becomes a major supporter and close friend of the artist (fig. 17). At this time, Miller acquires *Whirlpool Terrace*, a landscape box-sculpture, which later becomes a central piece in his home in Reading, Pennsylvania, designed by Kallmann McKinnell & Wood Architects of Boston, Massachusetts. The architects and Higby later collaborate on four major projects.

1988

Receives his third National Endowment for the Arts Visual Artists Fellowship grant.

Sixth solo exhibition with Helen W. Drutt English, which marks fifteen years of collaboration, opens at the Helen Drutt Gallery, New York, on October 29 (fig. 16).

16

17

1989

Receives a New York Foundation for the Arts Fellowship grant.

Work enters permanent collection of The National Museum of Modern Art, Tokyo, Japan.

Delivers lecture "The Driving Force in Craft Art: Concept or Material," Renwick Gallery, National Museum of American Art, Smithsonian Institution.

Elected president of the board of trustees, Haystack Mountain School of Crafts, Maine. Begins working closely with Stuart Kestenbaum, the newly appointed director of Haystack, who becomes a lifelong friend.

Appointed in overview panel, National Endowment for the Arts: Visual Arts Program, Washington, D.C.

Authors the article "The Intellectual and Sensual Pleasures of Utility" for *American Crafts* 49/1. An excerpt:

Fabricating an object of absolute utility, one that is the unique and ultimate solution to a given functional problem, is next to, if not completely, impossible. This is important to understand because often absolute utility is seen as the correct, most relevant goal of the functional potter. A potter's work may be criticized because it is not perfectly functional when, in fact, although it is amusing to attempt the impossible, such perfection is not the aim. Function is open to interpretation and it is in the arena of interpretation that the potter plays the game of creating for use.

Meets Sunkoo Yuh at NCECA, Kansas City, Missouri. Sunkoo later becomes an MFA student at Alfred and eventually a close, long-time friend and artist colleague.

1990

Receives the Master Teacher Award from the University of Hartford, Connecticut. To mark the occasion, he delivers the lecture "Art: Bridging the Space Between." Exhibits selected works at the art school's gallery.

Reappointed to the Visual Arts Program overview panel while serving on the advisory panel for Art's Education for the National Endowment for the Arts.

Exhibition Anne Currier and Wayne Higby, Pewabic Pottery, Detroit, Michigan.

One-person exhibition at the Helen Drutt Gallery, New York. Writing for the catalogue essay, Robert Turner observes:

The large bowl, which originated about 1975, represented for him a classic, universal object. By the increase of abstraction and simplicity of shape, it is less immediately accessible than the containers but becomes more powerful in effect, capturing and moving real space. Higby has the ability to carry that drama of image through a concurrent interacting of illusory and real dimension. With an uninterrupted oval sweep, the bowl allows color and line to have an abstract character. Now the flow of cloud over rim brings an added illusion of sensing all views as one, achieving a more than visual unity of landscape…. Indeed the illusion of the present and the infinite at once is haunting.

1991

Travels to Beijing, China, as a result of an invitation to be a speaker and one of six invited guests for the 1991 Beijing International Ceramic Art Convention, the first conference on contemporary ceramic art to be held in China, at the North China University of Technology, Beijing. Meets ceramic artist Yao Yongkang who eventually becomes an important friend—"Chinese Brother." Returns to the United States via Japan where he attends the opening of the Shigaraki Ceramic Culture Park and is introduced to many members of the International Academy of Ceramics.

Dewoo Corporation, located in South Korea, acquires five pieces for the Museum of Contemporary Art and the Hilton International Hotel, Gyeongju. They include *Morning Light Beach*, 1990, a landscape bowl; *Twist Rock Bay*, 1990, landscape bowl; *Noon Tide Beach*, 1990, landscape bowl; *Eventide Beach: View 3*, 1990, tile sculpture.

Featured speaker at the Haystack Mountain School of Craft's symposium *Craft in the 90's: A Return to Materials*. Excerpt from the presentation "Expectation: Art, Materials and the Photograph":

Are images of the work more important than the work itself? Is the messy material stuff just an inconvenient means to produce the slide? Without question, photography has become the principal venue through which art is promoted and sold. Has it also become the measure of the work?… It is one thing to be concerned about photography as the measure of the work or product. Another, far more serious concern, is that in many cases the photograph may be the measure of the making.

Speaker and panelist for "The Art of Collecting," sponsored by *American Ceramics* magazine, New York.

Philadelphia Museum of Art acquires landscape bowl *Idolon Bay*, 1986.

Denver Art Museum acquires landscape bowl *Snow at Red Mesa*, 1979, a gift of Paterson Sims.

In Tokyo, Ceramic Society of Japan acquires landscape bowl *Green Chrome Bay*, 1988.

Jiangsu Pictorial Art Monthly, China's premier art magazine at the time, publishes the work *Midnight Beach*, 1988, on its cover (fig. 18).

Juror for the inaugural Pew Foundation Fellowships in the Arts, grants to visual artists.

Juries *Anticipation '91* for emerging artists for the New Art Forms, SOFA, Chicago.

1992

Travels with wife Donna to China at the invitation of the Hubei Academy of Fine Arts, Wuhan, and the Jingdezhen Ceramic Institute, Jingdezhen. Extensive country travel for four weeks during May and June. Writer and coordinator for exhibition catalogue *5×7: Seven Ceramic Artists Acknowledge Five Sources of Inspiration*, Division of Ceramic Art, Alfred University.

Invited to be a visiting artist at the Nova Scotia College of Art and Design, Halifax, and Pennsylvania State University, State College.

1993

Takes a one-year sabbatical leave. Begins to work on *Intangible Notch*, a raku-fired tile installation for Arrow International, Reading, Pennsylvania. Commissioned by owner Marlin Miller in collaboration with Kallmann McKinnell & Wood Architects.

Travels to Lake Powell in southwestern Utah and returns with over a hundred sketches and photographs, which eventually inspire his work in porcelain (fig. 19).

1994

Travel and lecture tour of China and Taiwan; spends time speaking with artists, students, and faculty in Taipei, Tsaotun, and Nantou as well as South China Normal University, Guangzhou; Zhejiang Academy of Fine Arts, Hangzhou; Nanjing Academy of Fine Arts, Nanjing; and East China Normal University, Shanghai (fig. 20).

Visiting artist at the Jingdezhen Ceramic Institute, Jingdezhen, China; lectures and teaches for a week, including Freshman Foundation as well as advanced ceramic sculpture classes.

Strategizes and formulates an exchange agreement between Alfred University and the Jingdezhen Ceramic Institute.

Becomes an honorary professor at Jingdezhen Ceramic Institute, Jingdezhen, China.

In his 1993 to 1994 sabbatical report the artist articulates his thoughts on his initial involvement with China:

I felt privileged to have been invited to Jingdezhen … what I brought to them was essentially only one idea—first given formal articulation in Philadelphia, 1776. That idea is individual rights … freedom, "the pursuit of happiness," America's gift to mankind. It lies at the heart and soul of American art. What they gave me was insight into the critical nature of that idea and into the marrow of human resilience.

They renewed my belief in the urgent disposition of the creative act in and for itself. Eventually, it is from that grain, partical of sand, seed, that worlds are made and unmade. They confirmed my belief in art as communication—a meeting ground for global harmony.

Meets Mao Jianxiong, a scholar of Chinese art history at South China Normal University, who, over the years, becomes the artist's close friend and traveling companion.

Visiting artist address for the Taipei Ceramic Art Association, Museum of Fine Arts, Taipei.

Alfred Now: Contemporary American Ceramics, includes Alfred University's faculty members Anne Currier, Val Cushing, Andrea Gill, John Gill, and Wayne Higby at the Krannert Art Museum, Champaign, Illinois. Catalogue essayists include Donald Kuspit and Nancy Weekly.

Builds an addition to his home for a drawing studio.

Meets Lee Somers as freshman art student at Alfred. Lee eventually becomes a close friend and important collaborative assistant on several projects.

Begins his initial research into the possibilities of working in porcelain.

19

20

1995

Recognized as one of the "Vision-aries of the American Craft Move-ment," American Craft Museum (Museum of Arts and Design), New York.

Named founding member and international advisor to the Jingdezhen Kaolin Ceramic Art Association, China.

Travels to China, serves as Vice Chairman of the Jingdezhen Inter-national Ceramic Art conference. Conference sponsored by the United Nations Develop program for China.

Completes the 130 square foot installation of *Intangible Notch* at Arrow International headquarters.

Facilitates grant from Asian Cultural Council, New York, to bring artist Guanghui Chen to study ceramics at Alfred University; Chen is later appointed the head of ceramic art at Shanghai University, China.

1996

Writes catalogue essay "Walter Ostrom: Don't You Know," for exhibition *Walter Ostrom: The Advocacy of Pottery*, Art Gallery of Nova Scotia, Halifax.

His first presentation of a series of porcelain works is exhibited both at the Helen Drutt Gallery at Sculptural Objects Functional Art (SOFA) in Chicago and later at the Helen Drutt Gallery, Philadelphia.

1997

Wayne Higby: Tile Sculpture: 1996–1997, presented at the Helen Drutt Gallery, Philadelphia.

Daughter Sarah marries David Morabito on July 19; ceremony and reception held at the Higby farm complex. Close friend Stuart Kestenbaum, director of the Hay-stack Mountain School of Craft, presides and writes poem for the couple.

Meets Linda Sikora at her interview for a teaching position at the Division of Ceramic Art, School of Art and Design, Alfred University, New York. She becomes an impor-tant friend and colleague.

1998

Travels to China with selected students from across the United States. Attends the dedication of The Sanbao International Ceramic Art Institute, Jingdezhen, estab-lished by Li Jianshen (Jackson Lee; Alfred MFA 1995), China's first private ceramic art work center. Higby is named Honorary President.

Serves as the Honorary Chairperson at the first International Yixing Ceramic Art Conference. Travels with Jianxiong Mao on journey into the Three Gorges of China.

The Alfred University Division of Ceramic Art faculty receives the Friends of Contemporary Ceramics CLAY Award for lifetime achievement.

Writes and presents citation to artist Peter Voulkos, the recipient of an honorary doctorate of fine arts, Alfred University. Higby is respon-sible for conceptualizing and facili-tating this event, which included Voulkos's friend Robert Turner (figs. 21, 22).

The Metropolitan Museum of Art organizes exhibition *Clay Into Art: Contemporary Ceramics*. The work *Moon Water Bay*, 1990, a landscape bowl, is acquired from the exhibition.

Elected to the Council of Directors of the International Academy of Ceramics, Geneva, Switzerland. General Assembly meeting in Waterloo, Canada.

21

22

1999

Granddaughter, Olivia Claire Morabito, is born August 17. Travels to Finland, Russia, England, the Netherlands, and Switzerland. Visits St. Petersburg and wife's childhood homes in England, gives presentation at the Ceramic Millennium conference in Amsterdam and meets with the IAC in Geneva. Attends opening of his one-person show at the Taideteollisuuomuseo (Museum of Art and Design) in Helsinki, Finland, organizes the solo exhibition *Wayne Higby: Landscape as Memory 1990–1999*; a catalogue is published.

Work included in the exhibition *Choice from America: Modern American Ceramics*, featuring the Museum Kruithuis Collection at the Museum Paleis Lange Voorhout, The Hague, the Netherlands. Museum Het Kruithuis (Stedelijk Museum of Art), 's-Hertogenbosch, the Netherlands, acquires two landscape bowls: *South Park*, 1997, and *Rim Lake, Maurice's View*, 1982. *Disciple's Bay*, 1999, a tile sculpture, is featured on the cover of *Ceramics Art and Perception* 36.

Writes the introduction to Bai Ming, *The Spirit of Modern World Ceramic Art*, Jianzsu Publishing House, Beijing, China.

The artist is commissioned by the Metropolitan Museum of Art for the lecture-essay *Contemporary Ceramic Art, Folklore and Fact: The Legend of Alfred*. Excerpt from the essay:

What was the Alfred vessel? In 1973 [when I joined the faculty] I was unfamiliar with Garth's [Garth Clark's] term—perhaps he hadn't invented it yet. In my mind Alfred was much more than a particular kind of pot. Alfred was a place where the theory of art and design in ceramics found a scholarly home at the beginning of this century—a place that gave structure to the debate concerning what is best in ceramic art. It was a place where information and the "know how" was located, developed and generously shared so that ceramic art could grow and flourish across the United States.

Presented with a "Twenty-Five Year Citation" at Alfred University's Honors Convocation.

Presents the essay "If the Taj Mahal Was Made of Glass" at the Ceramic Millennium Conference, Amsterdam, the Netherlands. Excerpt from the presentation:

Imagine a Taj Mahal made of glass. In my mind's eye I see a structure formed out of sheets of hard transparent material linked together by a network of fine connecting ribs of support. From a distance it appears to be a mirage—illusionary, without substance—radiating a reflected light that is blinding in its intensity … hot, on fire, like a star falling to earth. Bright, crystalline luminosity—such an architecture might suggest the housing of a radiant energy and bring forth a theological meaning. What then of romantic love, longing and caressing sensuality, poetically transformed into ecstasy and peace? Glass—no, that is another universe, a different place, a manifestation of a different idea.

The Taj Mahal tells us unequivocally that making art is a triangular affair involving material, process, and idea. Whether it be music, dance, architecture, sculpture, or digital imaging, there exists a synergetic relationship between these three. This relationship provides a context for evaluation that reveals meaning.

2000

Travels to China, Tibet, and Germany. Participates at conferences in Jingdezhen as well as Foshan, China, and spends two weeks on a journey to Tibet (fig. 23). Attends IAC conference in Frechen, Germany. Gives the keynote address at *The Spirit of Porcelain* symposium, in conjunction with the international survey exhibition by the same title, held at the Jingdezhen Ceramic Institute, Jingdezhen, China. Excerpt from the address:

The ring of porcelain echoes against the walls of history taking the listener back through time a thousand years. The Jingdezhen of old comes alive. Dust clouds up from the red earth and wood smoke from a hundred kilns fills the air.

Something white, hard, pure, translucent, and brilliant in the light is being born from the heat of imagination. It is vitality, the invention of a belief, a principle of perfection. It is the Spirit of Porcelain. News travels around the world and across the centuries. Stories are told and retold about the kaolin and the fire. We learn of them today and are fascinated by the timeless enchantment of science and artistic vision. In our imagination and memory we celebrate the legend of Jingdezhen. We become a part of it. We become the Spirit of Porcelain.

Keynote speaker at the 1st International Ceramics Wood Firing Conference, Foshan, China; introduces American raku-firing process to China. Five hundred people attend nighttime demonstration. Is made Honorary Professor of Fine Arts, Shanghai University, China; a tree was planted in honor of the occasion.

Memorial Art Gallery, Rochester, New York, acquires *Entry Gate Creek*, a tile sculpture made in 1999, which in 2002 becomes cover image for book on the September 11, 2001, World Trade Center attack.

23

2001

Takes sabbatical leave for a year. Travels to South Korea and China. During a winter visit to Jingdezhen, selects work for the exhibition *Contemporary Jingdezhen Porcelain*, presented at the KOKO Gallery, New York, and the website gallery guild.com. This is the first time the work of leading contemporary Jingdezhen ceramic artists is seen in the United States.

Speaker and essayist for the exhibition *Earth and Fire: The Obscurity of the Obvious*, in conjunction with the World Ceramics Exposition 2001 Korea, International Ceramic Symposium *Measure the Immeasurable*, Ichon, South Korea.

The major exhibition *Color and Fire: Defining Moments in Studio Ceramics, 1950–2000* is organized by the Los Angeles County Museum of Art. Two works, *Flat Rock Falls*, 1979, landscape bowl and *Lake Powell Memory—Seven Mile Canyon*, 1996, a tile sculpture, are included. Develops the plan for the fireplace surround for Wingspread (designed by Frank Lloyd Wright) guesthouse, at the invitation of the Wingspread Foundation in Racine, Wisconsin. The project was never realized (fig. 25).

Wayne Higby: Landscape as Memory. A Retrospective is exhibited in his hometown at the Colorado Springs Fine Arts Center.

Receives a grant from Asian Cultural Council, New York, to bring Chunmao Huang from China to study at Alfred University. Huang, an Alfred MFA graduate in 2003, is head of Alfred—Central Academy of Fine Arts (CAFA) Ceramic Design for Industry program in Beijing, China.

Begins work on the monumental site project *EarthCloud* with assistant Lee Somers and technician Don Kaake. Commissioned by Marlin Miller for the Miller Performing Arts Building, Alfred University; project architects were Kallmann McKinnell & Wood Architects.

An excerpt from his sabbatical report demonstrates the importance of the commission:

There is no doubt that 2001–2002 was a very significant year for me. I worked hard in my studio. *Earth-Cloud* will see me into the future. I confronted the most puzzling questions regarding life and death, found new relevance in my recent sculpture, and returned to the original inspiration for my career as a ceramic artist.

2002

His son, Austin, suffers a near fatal motorcycle accident resulting in long-term disabilities.

Is presented the James Renwick Alliance Board of Governors Distinguished Educator Award, Renwick Gallery, Smithsonian American Art Museum.

Travels to Berlin to study the Ishtar Gate and to Greece to attend the biannual General Assembly of the IAC. Revisits Crete and the Heraklion Museum. The collection of Minoan pottery was his original inspiration to be a potter on his visit in 1963 at the age of twenty. In an excerpt from the Smithsonian Archives of American Art 2005 interview with art historian Mary Drach McInnes, the artist reflected:

We walked into this museum; it was almost exactly the way it was. Nothing had been changed and I found myself staring into the glass cases, looking at these pieces that I had seen when I was twenty years old.... At one point, I caught my reflection in the glass ... it was like the ghost of Christmas past ... I'm sixty years old and my twenty year-old persona is standing next to me looking through the same glass window at the same pot ... a wonderful

kind of revelation about how this twenty-year-old kid who knew absolutely nothing about anything, actually knew something ... The sixty year old said: "Kid, pretty sharp. This is hot stuff."

Entry Gate Creek, 1999, a tile sculpture, is the cover feature for *September 11, 2001: American Writers Respond* (fig. 24). Edited by William Heyden. Published by Etruscan Press, Heyden wrote about the artist's *Entry Gate Creek*:

When walking through the Memorial Art Gallery in Rochester, I first saw Wayne Higby's sculpture; I was lost in it, rapt with it. I pressed my face against the Lucite box that held it. I couldn't get close enough to it. I looked at it from all sides, absorbed by it, its strength, its burnished beauty, its sense of ruin, its ever-unfolding depths. I felt in it peacefulness, after the tragic, against a crackled sky—nature's waters and landscape and human emotion fused. The sculpture now keeps on giving of itself to me, seems to be a place beneath my breastbone, after Ground Zero, the place where we are as we dwell on September 11.

In response to Heyden's observations, the artist, in his 2001–2002 sabbatical report wrote:

Heyden's emotional response to my work moved me profoundly and has triggered a renewed contemplation of the meanings housed within my art. I returned to the tile sculpture.

Serves as an advisor for the Smithsonian's *Silk Road Celebration*, The Mall, Washington, D.C.

2003

Grandson Oscar Wray Morabito is born March 8.

Wayne Higby: Thresholds, one-person exhibition at Burchfield Penney Art Center, Buffalo, New York, with catalogue.

Elected Lifetime Trustee, Haystack Mountain School of Crafts.

Teaches junior-level ceramic sculpture class and meets student Ian McMahon. Ian eventually becomes a close friend and collaborative assistant.

Accepts commission from Robert L. McNeil to design and produce Alfred University award for the outstanding senior male and female undergraduate to be awarded annually in honor of Marlin Miller.

2004

Grandson Owen Caspar Morabito is born September 23.

Wife of thirty-eight years, Donna Claire Higby, dies of ovarian cancer.

Travels to China to attend conference in Jingdezhen and to South Korea for the General Assembly meeting of the IAC.

Elected vice president of the International Academy of Ceramics, Geneva, at the General Assembly held in Icheon, South Korea.

Is recognized as Honorary Citizen of Jingdezhen, China. This is the first time a foreign national has become an honorary citizen of Jingdezhen. The award is presented by the Mayor of Jingdezhen at a banquet held in the artist's honor on May 28 and was part of the Millennium Anniversary of Jingdezhen; Jingdezhen was declared the Imperial Kiln Site of China in 1004. Presents the keynote address "Education Is Not a Country" for the International Ceramic Art Education Conference in Jingdezhen. In his essay for the catalogue, he writes:

The dynamic of educational exchange that has been established here in Jingdezhen is not only about China and the West or the West and China. Much more importantly, a universal example has been established—an example that instructs our understanding of mutual interest—an example that illuminates both art and life—an example that encour-

ages us to always try to communicate even when we have no words.

I traveled to Jingdezhen for the first time in 1992. I was forty-eight years old, an acknowledged American master of ceramic art and a well-established university professor. I spoke no Chinese, but I had reason to believe I was an educated man. I had much to learn. Jingdezhen taught me that not only was education not a country, education was also not simply money in the bank. Jingdezhen taught me that education was always present in the moment, in the everyday experiences of life. Education was alive, truly happening, breathing in every second of existence. Much of my thinking about art and life began to change, to confirm, to develop, back then in 1992. I found renewed use for my accomplishments and a revived sense of educational purpose. I became a better teacher, a better artist, a better listener, a better friend. I became more compassionate, more informed, more fulfilled. Now, I look forward to each return visit to Jingdezhen for I know I will be expanded in some unexpected way. Education is always about nurturing the imagination. Jingdezhen has without question done that for me.

First meeting with Pan Gonkai, president of the Central Academy of Fine Arts (CAFA), Beijing. The initial discussion of an Alfred University (AU)-CAFA ceramic art partnership took place at Alfred University; a 2005 meeting in Beijing became a solid step toward developing a collaborative program. In time a studio was built on the CAFA City Design School campus, thus launching the AU-CAFA Ceramic Design for Industry program, which was formally established in 2006 and officially dedicated in 2008.

2005

Traveling to Thailand and Cambodia and retracing steps of his wander-jahre student trip of 1963, the artist returns to the Temples of Angkor Siem Reap, Cambodia.

Also gives a workshop at the Central Academy of Fine Arts, Beijing, China, and travels to Kecskemét, Hungary, for the IAC council meeting.

Diagnosed with colon cancer; with surgery successful, spends eight weeks recovering.

Is named the Robert Chapman Turner Chair of Ceramic Art, the first honorary chair position in the School of Art and Design at Alfred University. The chair is named after the highly esteemed Alfred University artist-educator Robert Turner (fig. 26).

Receives the Honors of the Council award, honorary member of the National Council on Education for the Ceramic Arts. Fellow Alfred faculty member John Gill makes the introductory remarks at the NCECA conference in Baltimore, Maryland.

Is presented the James Renwick Alliance Board of Governors Master of the Media award, Renwick Gallery, Smithsonian American Art Museum.

Art historian Mary Drach McInnes conducts an oral history with the artist for the Smithsonian Archives of American Art.

Develops and facilitates with Professor Anne Currier the *Material Matters* exhibition, held at the Fosdick-Nelson Gallery at Alfred University. There is an accompanying catalogue.

Continues to work on the *Earth-Cloud* commission.

Meets Hongwei Li in Beijing, China. Hongwei eventually becomes a close friend and collaborative assistant on architectural projects.

Important friend and mentor Robert Turner dies.

26

2006

Travels to China to facilitate the opening of the Alfred Ceramic Design for Industry program at the Central Academy of Fine Arts, Beijing, and to oversee the final phase of the construction of the studio classroom. Later travels to Stuttgart, Germany, to attend meetings with the art publisher Arnoldsche in connection with the design and production of the book on *EarthCloud*. Commissioned for the Miller Performing Arts Building at Alfred University, the first part of *EarthCloud* is completed after five years in development and production; it comprises approximately 6,000 hand-cut celadon-glazed porcelain tiles and is thirty feet high and sixty feet wide. In his statement for the book published on *EarthCloud* the artist writes: *EarthCloud*, I can't remember when that title came to me, but it describes an abiding theme in my work from the beginning. Earth, of course, is the drama of material, weight, gravity—the tactile, the sensual matrix of human life.

We are of the earth and are bound by our bodies, as products of nature revealed in the phenomena of the physical universe. Yet, we are also of the transcendent—the purely imagined possibility of mind. At once real, grounded, but as well free to move deeply into imaginary realms, we are *EarthCloud*.

Develops a detailed curriculum and writes the official agreement documents to establish the AU-CAFA Ceramic Design for Industry program in collaboration with the Central Academy of Fine Arts, Beijing. Begins inspiring relationship with Dr. Lisa Lantz, a concert violinist, conductor, and professor of music at Alfred University (fig. 27). Classical music becomes an important fact of life.

Meets Benjamin DeMott as a first-year MFA student. Benjamin eventually becomes a close friend, collaborative assistant, and critical factor in the success of the architectural projects. In honor of Robert Turner, the SOFA catalogue includes *Recalling Bob Turner: Finding the Words*, an essay reflecting on his passing. Higby begins his essay with a poem by Wen Chao in tenth-century China:

We meet
To part again
I have no words
To respond
To this double
Inspiration.

27

2007

Takes a sabbatical leave for a year to develop new architectural project for the Miller Center for the Arts, Reading, Pennsylvania.

Travels to Switzerland for the IAC council meeting as well as to Beijing to review the AU-CAFA program and to Thailand for an adventurous week on the island of Kol Tao in the Bay of Thailand with friends Lee and Elisabeth Sommers and collaborative assistant Ian McMahon.

New Year's Eve party held in the artist's honor at the Ancient Kiln site in Foshan, China; re-enacts his raku demonstration from 2000.

Receives the Joseph Kruson Faculty Award for distinguished service to Alfred University and designated a Kruson Distinguished Professor. Formal dedication of the *EarthCloud* installation at Alfred University. In his dedication speech, the artist speaks about his early interests in art:

My experience as an adolescent was perhaps fairly typical for a young artist. Of course, I didn't know I was an artist or would become one. I did feel emotionally isolated from the general societal expectations of life, school, etc. My world was materials: paint, paper, sticks, clay. We communicated. It was a collaboration through which I was given the gift of self-realization. I learned that art was really a cooperative endeavor in which a respect for earthborn materials revealed resonance and truth. *EarthCloud*, a one-person exhibition at the Fosdick-Nelson Gallery,

Alfred University tracking the development of the *EarthCloud* project includes retrospective examples of related earlier work. The monograph *EarthCloud* is published by Arnoldsche Art Publishers, Stuttgart.

His essay for the book includes a reference to the inspiration gained by visiting the temples of Angkor: Forty-two years later in January 2005 while I was in the final stages of making *EarthCloud*, I returned to Angkor [first visited in 1963]. The first evening of my return … I stood completely transfixed by the grand façade of Angkor Wat, utterly timeless in the fading light. It was then I realized with certain comprehension that I had carried the Temples of Angkor across the years buried deep within my imagination.… All those years ago at the age of twenty-one, long before I chose ceramics as a medium and long before I became fully conscious of my interest in architecture, I had unknowingly grasped in total mind-body wonder the necessities of my art …

At Angkor the mind-body equation is played out in vast, monumental architectural structure. Massive weight celebrating gravity is lifted up by the energy of intrinsic surface elaboration. The physical limits of structure are transformed into pure imagination where the complexities of mind give meaning to existence (fig. 29).

28

2008

On New Year's Day meets Manjian Chen, owner and director of Individuality Art Ceramics, an architectural tile factory located in the city of Foshan. They begin collaboration, resulting in a close friendship, as the project *SkyWell Falls* for the Miller Center for the Arts in Reading takes shape. *SkyWell Falls* will be fabricated in Manjian's factory.

Travels with Jianxiong Mao on a journey into China's Northwest Territory and visits the Buddhist caves at Dunhuang.

Gives the keynote address at the International Academy of Ceramics General Assembly meeting in Xian, China. Titled "kong.flux," the artist speaks about the significance of his time in China:

On May 20, 1994, I hosted a banquet and karaoke dance party for the faculty of the Jingdezhen Ceramic Institute. This was a small gesture of appreciation on my part, which turned out to be the party to end all parties as far as I was concerned. The month, the day, the year: the timing was right. Everyone danced and danced with everyone, no gender phobias. The older faculty, deeply experienced with the dynamics of Chinese life, found within themselves a youthful exuberance and, extending their permission and hope for the future, blended their spirits with the chemistry of optimism. The companionship of the moment was golden. Everyone was welcoming a new voltage of possibility. Events like this one may have occurred elsewhere in China in the early 1990s, but they were not commonplace. It was a very special time in China, in Jingdezhen, in Chinese ceramic art. It was a very special time in my life. If you are truly open to experience, nothing is really surprising, but everything does make you wonder. That is why I keep coming back to China. There is always something more, some contradiction I need explained, something deeper that I want to understand. I'm curious, fascinated, and bewildered by China. Perhaps, it is more profoundly true that in the search for myself, China has been my guide, my teacher and, like a schoolboy, I have fallen in love with my teacher.

Manhattan Canyon, a commission for Bob McComsey, is completed and installed (fig. 28).

2009

Travels to China numerous times as he continues research and development for the *SkyWell Falls* project for the Miller Center for the Arts; spends two months at the factory in Foshan, China, working with personal assistants Benjamin DeMott, Hongwei Li, and Tom Schmidt as well as the factory technicians and craftsmen.

SkyWell Falls is installed during the late summer and dedicated on December 4 (fig. 30).

Attends the exhibition for the first class of graduating students from the Alfred-CAFA Ceramic Design for Industry program, Beijing.

Receives the Peter Voulkos Visiting Artist Fellowship at the Archie Bray Foundation for the Ceramic Arts.

Spends two weeks in residence developing new work with the help of collaborative assistant Benjamin DeMott.

Invited to install the exhibit *Wayne Higby: Landscapes*, a one-person exhibition, Cosmos Club, Washington, D.C.

Appointed honorary director of the Institute of International Arts, South China Normal University, Guangzhou, China.

Meets Mahlon Huston as a first-year MFA student. Mahlon eventually becomes a close friend and collaborative assistant helping to finish the final phase of *EarthCloud* and prepare for the Higby retrospective.

Travels to Switzerland for the IAC council meeting.

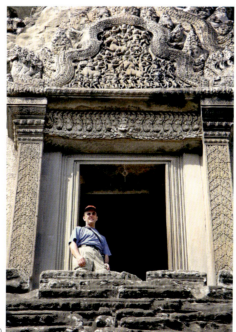

29

30

2010

Travels to Guangzhou, China, to make a presentation at the conference-symposium *Art in the Digital Age*, South China Normal University, and then travels extensively in the Yunnan province with Jianxiong Mao, Hongwei Li, and Tanya Harrod. Returns to the United States via Prague, Czech Republic, to study its architecture and later returns to Europe to attend the IAC General Assembly in Paris.

First design phase, and pre- and postproduction for the expanded development of *EarthCloud* begins. Commissioned by Marlin Miller for the new Miller Theater, an addition to the Miller Performing Arts Building at Alfred University. Collaborates with Kallmann McKinnell & Wood Architects as well as personal studio collaborators Benjamin DeMott and Lee Somers, and technician Don Kaake.

Is invited to be guest curator for the Scripps College 66th Ceramic Annual; the exhibition is *Material Matters: Art and Phenomena*.

For his catalogue essay, he writes:
The concept that all art is based in phenomena and must be experienced via the senses prior to any

historical, sociopolitical, biographical, or psychological reading may seem obvious. However, it refutes an assumption that has ruled art theory since the early twentieth century: that idea is the single most important aspect of works of art. From the moment in 1917 that Marcel Duchamp transposed a common urinal into an art context and thereby raised fundamental philosophical questions about the origins of art, sensory perception became suspect as a means to judge art and, as a result, concept was elevated to an a priori status by most critics. This teaching supports the notion that quality work derives exclusively from stimulation of the intellect. Intellect has come to mean mind separate from the body; relying on the senses to interpret the phenomena of experience is no longer a primary contingency of perception. Art theory has superseded the work itself. Rarely do we read serious critique that incorporates intelligent insight into the necessities of material and process in facilitating ideas. Nevertheless, I believe that the fusion of material–idea–process leads to meaning in works of art.

In the opening night address of "Art and Expectation," his presentation offers advice on the potential of art and perception:
Our potential to learn, to grow in perception and understanding is facilitated or hampered by expectation. If our encounter with art is predicated on expecting confirmation for what we already know, then the potential of refreshed or new insight is eliminated.
Set aside the need to know. Set aside the drive to understand. Set aside what has been said, written, assumed. Critical observer, amateur, or professional—stop thinking long enough for the senses to take hold, for experience to rise up out of a sensual resonance to embrace intellectual revelation. Then add the background, the history, and the biographical data—what is known already.

Tower Lands Winter, 1988, a landscape container, is chosen as the book cover for Barbara Lovenheim, *Breaking Ground: A Century of Craft Art in Western New York*, published by The Memorial Art Gallery, Rochester, New York, and Hudson Hills Press, Manchester, Vermont.

Begins development of a new branding concept for Individuality Art Ceramics, Foshan, China, at the request of factory owner and director, Manjian Chen. This entails a new logo and a comprehensive redesign of a visual standards manual. Concepts are made in collaboration with graphic designer Rick McLay.

Grant awarded by the Windgate Charitable Foundation to mount a retrospective with curator Peter Held, Arizona State University Art Museum, Tempe.

2011

The monograph *SkyWell Falls* is published, providing an overview of the conceptualization, production, and installation of the project for the Miller Center for the Arts. Essays by art historian Mary Drach McInnes and the artist are included.

Excerpt from Higby's essay:
As a professor of art, I am often confronted by the question: What is the difference between an art and design? After all, I teach at the School of Art and Design at Alfred University. My answer to the question: An artist invents the problem where, in fact, there is no problem and then proposes/achieves a solution. The designer accepts an already existing problem and proposes/achieves a solution. Each requires a special gift. Each relies heavily on the other. I think of myself first and foremost as an artist, but in addressing the challenge of an architectural reality, I must rely on my intuition as a designer.

Work continues on the production of the hand-cut tiles for the new *EarthCloud* project for the Miller Theater, eventually taking two years to complete.

Becomes honorary alumnus at Alfred University.

Travels to China regularly at this point in connection with his ongoing work at the Central Academy of Fine Arts, Beijing.

31

2012

Travels to China to oversee Alfred-CAFA program and to Havana, Cuba, to survey the dynamics of Cuban ceramic art, art, architecture, and culture.

Continues teaching full time, marking the thirty-ninth year of teaching at Alfred University. Courses include beginner- and advanced-level undergraduate ceramics as well as a graduate student studio and two graduate student seminars, one of which deals with issues in contemporary art which he has facilitated for students in Ceramic Art and Sculpture for over twenty years.

Made honorary member, Chinese Ceramic Art Masters League at their meeting in Shanghai, China. Emotional reunion with close friend Yao Yongkang in Jingdezhen, China (fig. 31). In December of 2011, Yao Yongkang wrote of the history of the friendship. Yao Yongkang is a sculptor and professor emeritus of Jingdezhen University (the Jingdezhen Ceramic Institute). He is considered by many to be China's premier ceramic artist.

Yao Yongkang writes:
I met Wayne for the first time during the first Beijing Ceramic Art Seminar in 1991. The first impression of him was handsome, humorous, learned with high artistic achievements, and rather poetic. After that we became good friends. We were connected together based on our artworks. Our friendship became deeper. We understood each other despite the language barrier....
In those days [early 1990s], he was always surrounded by us ... he delivered speeches and we were drinking and dancing. When the bonfire ignited we were all crazy, crazy about ceramic art and also crazy about art. Could this kind of pure time come back again? The answer is no. It could not be brought back with gold and it seems that gold will not buy anything. This was art! Valuable art!
The final phase of EarthCloud is installed, culminating an eleven-year engagement with the project for the Miller Performing Arts Complex at Alfred University. Excerpt from a text in CenterStage,

newsletter of the Division of Performing Arts, Alfred University:
EarthCloud 2006/2012
EarthCloud is complete. The final phase of the installation took place during May, June, and July. A team of ten artists as well as members of the LeChase Construction Company, placed the last 6,000 tiles up on the wall of Miller Theater. The completed piece, which now flows between the Miller Performing Arts Building and Miller Theater, connects the two and, in total, is comprised of over 12,000 hand-cut porcelain tiles, encompassing close to 5,520 square feet of space....
EarthCloud creates a unique and often surprising fusion of art, architecture, and landscape. Most spectacular at night, the illuminated artwork manifests a continuum of real and illusionistic space as fact and reflection embrace each other in a rare expanded infinity of place. Revelatory, it confirms the Miller complex at Alfred University as a work of art and architecture of international stature.

The EarthCloud team, left to right beginning at the top: Wayne Higby, Mahlon Huston, Elliott Thorpe, Benjamin DeMott, Brian Caponi, Hongwei Li, Trevor Bennett, Lee Somers, Aaron Benson, Don Kaake, Nick Geankoplis (fig. 32).
Moon Water Bay, 1991, a landscape bowl, is selected for the installation of contemporary ceramic masterworks at the Metropolitan Museum of Art. Work is featured in the exhibition New "China": Porcelain Art from Jingdezhen 1910–2012, China Institute Gallery, China Institute, New York, N.Y. Exhibition includes the work of twenty-five Chinese artists and Higby. Catalogue entry notes:
Since his participation in the first conference on contemporary ceramic art, held in the Peoples' Republic of China in 1991, Wayne Higby has done more than anyone else to build bridges between contemporary Chinese and American ceramics.
Reappointed vice president of the International Academy of Ceramics, Geneva, at the General Assembly held in Santa Fe, New Mexico.

Selected Resume

Born 1943, Colorado Springs, Colorado

Education

1968	MFA, University of Michigan, Ann Arbor, Michigan
1966	BFA, University of Colorado Boulder, Colorado

Academic Appointments

1973–present	Professor, Robert C. Turner Chair of Ceramic Art, Alfred University, Alfred, New York
	Kruson Distinguished Professor, Alfred University, Alfred, New York
	Founding Director, ALFRED-CAFA Ceramic Design for Industry Program, Central Academy of Fine Arts, Beijing, China
1970–73	Assistant Professor, Rhode Island School of Design, Providence, Rhode Island
1968–70	Assistant Professor, University of Nebraska, Omaha, Nebraska

Selected Awards and Honors

2012	Honorary Member, Chinese Ceramic Art Masters League, Shanghai, China
2011	Honorary Alumnus, Alfred University, Alfred, New York
2010	Honorary Director of the Institute of International Arts, College of Fine Arts, South China Normal University, Guangzhou, China
2009	Voulkos Fellow, Archie Bray Foundation for the Ceramic Arts, Helena, Montana
2005	Honorary Member, National Council on Education for the Ceramic Arts
	Master of the Media, James Renwick Alliance, Smithsonian American Art Museum, Washington, D.C.
2004	Honorary Citizen, Jingdezhen, China
2003	Lifetime Trustee, Haystack Mountain School of Crafts, Deer Isle, Maine
2002	Distinguished Educator Award, James Renwick Alliance, Smithsonian American Art Museum, Washington, D.C.
	Honorary Professor of Art, College of Fine Arts, Shanghai University, China
1998	Recognition of Excellence, American Ceramic Society, Westerville, Ohio
	Friends of Contemporary Ceramics 3rd Annual Lifetime Achievement Award, for past and present Faculty of the Division of Ceramic Art, College of Ceramics at Alfred University, Alfred, New York
1995	American Craft Movement Visionary Award, American Craft Museum (Museum of Arts and Design), New York, N.Y.
	College of Fellows, American Craft Council, New York, N.Y.
	Honorary Professor of Ceramic Art, Jingdezhen Ceramic Institute, Jingdezhen, China
1993	Chancellor's Award for Excellence in Teaching, State University of New York, N.Y.
1990	Master Teacher Award, University of Hartford, Hartford, Connecticut
1986	George A. and Eliza Howard Foundation Fellowship, administered by Brown University, Providence, Rhode Island
1985, 1989	New York Foundation for the Arts Fellowship, New York, N.Y.
1976	National Parks Service Grant, National Parks Service, U.S. Department of the Interior, Washington, D.C.
1973, 1977, 1988	National Endowment for the Arts Fellowship, Washington, D.C.

Selected Solo Exhibitions

2013   *Infinite Place: The Ceramic Art of Wayne Higby*, a retrospective, two year traveling exhibition, organized by the Arizona State University
            Art Museum, Tempe, Arizona
2007   *Wayne Higby: The Making of EarthCloud*, Fosdick-Nelson Gallery, Alfred University, Alfred, New York
2003   *Wayne Higby: Thresholds*, Burchfield Penney Art Center, Buffalo, New York
2001   *Wayne Higby: Landscape as Memory, a Retrospective*, Colorado Springs Fine Arts Center, Colorado Springs, Colorado
1999   *Wayne Higby: Landscape as Memory, 1990–1999*, Design Museum, Helsinki, Finland
1997   *Wayne Higby*, Helen Drutt Gallery, Philadelphia, Pennsylvania (1997, 1996, 1982, 1980, 1979, 1978, 1976)
            Wayne Higby: New Work, Morgan Gallery, Kansas City, Missouri
            Wayne Higby: Porcelain, Helen Drutt Gallery, SOFA Chicago, Navy Pier, Chicago, Illinois
1991   Morgan Gallery, Kansas City, Missouri
1990   Helen Drutt Gallery, New York, N.Y.
            Hartford Art School, University of Hartford, Connecticut
1988   *Wayne Higby*, Helen Drutt Gallery, New York, N.Y.
1984   Greenwich House Pottery, New York, N.Y.
1980   Exhibit A, Evanston, Illinois (1980, 1978, 1975)
1979   Okun-Thomas Gallery, St. Louis, Missouri
1977   Yaw Gallery, Birmingham, Michigan
1973   *Wayne Higby: Ceramic Landscapes*, Museum of Contemporary Crafts (Museum of Arts and Design), New York, N.Y.
1971   Benson Gallery, Bridgehampton, Long Island, New York
1970   Archie Bray Foundation, Helena, Montana
1969   Joslyn Art Museum, Omaha, Nebraska

Selected Group Exhibitions

2012   *The Ambit of Embraces: Contemporary Ceramics*, Frank Lloyd Gallery, Santa Monica, California
            Around the Bend and Over the Edges: Seattle Ceramics 1964–1977, Henry Art Gallery, University of Washington, Seattle, Washington
            Infinite Echoes: Asian Ceramics and Global Traditions, Late 19th–21st Century, Metropolitan Museum of Art, New York, N.Y. (two-year installation)
            New China: Porcelain Art from Jingdezhen, 1910–2012, China Institute, New York, N.Y.
2011   *Then and Now*, Holter Museum of Art, Helena, Montana
2010   International Academy of Ceramics Invitational, Sèvres Ceramics Museum, Paris, France
            Let's Table This: A Survey of Table Top Vessels, American Museum of Ceramic Art, Pomona, California
            Spectra, Fosdick-Nelson Gallery, Alfred University, Alfred, New York
            Town and Country: Urban and Rural Scenes from RAM's Collection, Racine Art Museum, Racine, Wisconsin
2009   *A Passionate Observer: A Tribute to Helen Drutt*, The Clay Studio, Philadelphia, Pennsylvania
            Standing on the Shoulders of Giants, Columbus State University, Columbus, Georgia
            21st Century Iconographic Clayworks, Lindfield College, McMinnville, Oregon
2008   *Contemporary Studio Ceramics: The Dauer Collection*, California State University, Sacramento, California
            Haystack: Creative Process, Center for Community Programs, Deer Isle, Maine
2007   *Innovation and Change: Great Ceramics from the Permanent Collection*, Arizona State University Art Museum, Tempe, Arizona
            Craft in America: Expanding Traditions, national touring exhibition, opening at the Arkansas Art Center, Little Rock, Arkansas
            Craft in Context: The Dorothy and George Saxe Collection, M. H. de Young Memorial Museum, San Francisco, California
            Selections from the Annette Cravens Modern Ceramics Collection, Burchfield Penney Art Center, Buffalo, New York
2006   *Alfred Ceramics, The Henry Bauer Collection*, University Gallery, University of North Carolina, Asheville, North Carolina
2005   *East Meets West: The Contemporary Asian Aesthetic in RAM's Collection*, Racine Museum of Art, Racine, Wisconsin
            Inaugural Exhibition, Hurong Lou Gallery, Philadelphia, Pennsylvania

2004	*Artful Giving: Collector's Circle Acquisitions 1994–2004*, Renwick Gallery, Smithsonian American Art Museum, Washington, D.C.; Long Beach Museum of Art, Long Beach, California
	Jingdezhen Millennium of Porcelain International Ceramic Art Invitational, Jingdezhen Ceramic Institute, Jingdezhen, China
	Realism and Illusion, Colorado Springs Fine Art Center, Colorado Springs, Colorado
	Standing Room Only: The 60th Scripps Ceramic Annual, Scripps College, Claremont, California
2003	*Ceramic Masterworks*, Moderne Gallery, Philadelphia, Pennsylvania
	From the Collection: Selected New Gifts, Schein-Joseph International Museum of Ceramic Art, Alfred University, Alfred, New York
	Generations: Impending Lineage, Arts and Industry Gallery, San Diego, California
	Great Pots: Contemporary Ceramics from Function to Fantasy, Newark Museum, Newark, New Jersey
	Inaugural Exhibition, New Racine Art Museum, Racine, Wisconsin
	21st Century Ceramics in the United States and Canada, Columbus College of Art and Design, Columbus, Ohio
2002	*Ceramics National 2000*, Crocker Art Museum, Sacramento, California
	Coming of Age, Craft + Design Collection, Mint Museum, Charlotte, North Carolina
	Gifts in Honor of the 125th Anniversary, Philadelphia Museum of Art, Philadelphia, Pennsylvania
	Hellas 50th Anniversary Members Exhibition, International Academy of Ceramics, project of the Cultural Olympiad 2001–2004, Hellenic Ministry of Culture, Athens, Greece
2001	*Allan Chasanoff Ceramic Collection*, Craft + Design Collection, Mint Museum, Charlotte, North Carolina
	Ceramics as Sculpture: Challenging the Functional Tradition, Minneapolis Museum of Art, Minneapolis, Minnesota
	Haystack: Pivotal Transformations, Haystack Mountain School of Crafts, Deer Isle, Maine
	Poetics of Clay: An International Perspective, Philadelphia Art Alliance, Philadelphia, Pennsylvania
	Reunion: Wayne Higby and the MFA Graduates of Alfred University Ceramics Program, The Clay Studio, Philadelphia, Pennsylvania
	USA Clay, Renwick Gallery, Smithsonian American Art Museum, Washington, D.C.
	A View of Contemporary Ceramics, Chester Springs Studio, Chester Springs, Pennsylvania
	World Ceramics Exhibition 2001 Korea, International Academy of Ceramics, Choson Royal Kiln Museum, Kwangju, South Korea
2000	*Centennial Celebration, Division of Ceramic Art, New York State College of Ceramics at Alfred University*, American Ceramic Society Exposition, St. Louis, Missouri
	Color and Fire: Defining Moments in American Studio Ceramics 1950–2000, Los Angeles County Museum of Art, Los Angeles, California
	China Contemporary Ceramics, Shanghai New International Expo Center, Shanghai, China
	Everson Ceramic National 2000: 30th Ceramic National, Everson Museum of Art, Syracuse, New York
	Firing Cycle: Fifty Years of Clay at the Potters Guild, Slusser Gallery, Ann Arbor, Michigan
	International Ceramic Art Exhibition 2000, Shiwan Treasure Art Pottery Museum, Foshan, China
	Living with Form: The Horn Collection of Contemporary Crafts, Arkansas Art Center, Little Rock, Arkansas
	Not So Hidden Treasures, 1961–2000, Helen Drutt Gallery, Philadelphia, Pennsylvania
	Recent American Ceramics: Selections from the Everson Museum of Art, SUNY at Potsdam, New York
	Spaces: Interior and Exterior, The Clay Studio, Philadelphia, Pennsylvania
	The Spirit of Porcelain: International Survey of Ceramic Art, Jingdezhen Ceramic Institute, Jingdezhen, China
1999	*The Alfred Asia Connection: The Asia Alfred Reflection*, Taipei Gallery, New York, N.Y.
	Choice from America: Modern American Ceramics, Museum Het Kruithuis Collection at the Museum Paleis Lange Voorhout, The Hague, the Netherlands
	The Art of Craft: Works from the Saxe Collection, M. H. de Young Memorial Museum, San Francisco, California
	Contemporary New York State Crafts, New York State Museum, Albany, New York
	Earthenware: A Nova Scotia Tradition, Art Gallery of Nova Scotia, Halifax, Nova Scotia, Canada
	Twentieth Century Art at the Turn of the Millennium, Helen Drutt Gallery, Philadelphia, Pennsylvania
1998	*Clay Into Art: Contemporary Ceramics*, Metropolitan Museum of Art, New York, N.Y.
	Craft as a Verb, selections from the American Craft Museum (Museum of Arts and Design), Mississippi Museum of Art, Jacksonville, Mississippi
	Drawing on Clay, Baltimore Clayworks, Baltimore, Maryland
	5th International Triennial of Contemporary Porcelain, Chateau De Nyon, Nyon, Switzerland
	Night of 101 Cups, Garth Clark Gallery, New York, N.Y.
	Pittsburgh Collects Clay: Selection from Pittsburgh Collections, Carnegie Museum of Art, Pittsburgh, Pennsylvania
	Yixing International Ceramic Art, invitational exhibition, Yixing, China

1997   *Centennial Education Exhibition*, Society of Arts and Crafts, Boston, Massachusetts

Clay Traditions, Dallas Museum of Fine Arts, Dallas, Texas

Celebrating American Craft: 1975–1995, Det Danske Kunstrundustrimuseet (Museum of Decorative Arts), Copenhagen, Denmark

Collector's Choice: 1997, Colorado Springs Fine Art Center, Colorado Springs, Colorado

Contemporary New York State Crafts, New York State Museum, Albany, New York

Sculpture Objects Functional Art, SOFA Chicago, Navy Pier, Chicago, Illinois

1996   *Alfred Teaches Ceramics 1990–1996*, International Museum of Ceramic Art at Alfred University, Alfred, New York

From the Source: Diamond Celebration, 60th Anniversary Exhibition, Colorado Springs Fine Arts Center, Colorado Springs, Colorado

Mutual Affinities: Selections from the Aaron Milrad Collection, Castellani Art Museum, Niagara University, Niagara Falls, New York

Selections from the Robert Pfannebecker Collection, Hershey Museum, Hershey, Pennsylvania

1995   *Alfred Now: Contemporary American Ceramics. Anne Currier, Val Cushing, Andrea Gill, John Gill, and Wayne Higby*, Krannert Art Museum, Champaign, Illinois

Kaolin International Ceramic Art Exhibition, Jiangxi Porcelain Research Institute, Jingdezhen, China

1994   *About Face! (Figuratively Speaking)*, Innovation Center, Alfred University, Alfred, New York

KPMG Peat Warwick Collection of American Craft: A Gift to the Renwick Gallery, Smithsonian American Art Museum, Washington, D.C.

1993   *American Crafts: The Nation's Collection, Twentieth Anniversary Exhibition*, Renwick Gallery, Smithsonian American Art Museum, Washington, D.C.

Contemporary Craft and the Saxe Collection, Toledo Museum of Art, Toledo, Ohio; Saint Louis Art Museum, St. Louis, Missouri; Newport Harbor Art Museum, Newport Beach, California

Working With Tradition: The Academic Artist, Burchfield Art Center, State University College at Buffalo, New York; New York State Museum, Albany, New York

Archie Bray Teapot Benefit Exhibit, International Gallery, San Diego, California

Contemporary American Ceramics: 1980 to the Present, Stetson University, DeLand, Florida

Local Clay Samples, SUNY Brockport, Brockport, New York; Burchfield Art Center, Buffalo, New York

New Acquisitions, The National Museum of Modern Art, Tokyo, Japan

Working in Other Dimensions: Objects and Drawings, Arkansas Art Center, Little Rock, Arkansas

The Year of American Craft: 1993, Maveety Gallery, Portland, Oregon

100th Anniversary Celebration, Denver Art Museum, Denver, Colorado

1992   *A Salute to the Haystack Mountain School of Crafts: Works by Faculty*, Society of Arts and Crafts, Boston, Massachusetts

The Archie Bray Foundation, Helen Drutt Gallery, New York, N.Y.

The Cachepot: Revisiting the Decorative "Pot Hider", Swidler Gallery, Royal Oak, Michigan

Chthonic Realms: Philadelphia Collects Clay, Helen Drutt Gallery, Philadelphia, Pennsylvania

Inaugural Exhibition, Okun Gallery, Santa Fe, New Mexico

Twentieth Century Ceramics, Los Angeles County Museum of Art, Pacific Design Center, Los Angeles, California

1991   *Collecting American Decorative Art and Sculpture 1971–1991*, Museum of Fine Arts, Boston, Massachusetts

Minor Works by Major Artists, Arizona State University Art Museum, Tempe, Arizona

Seventeen Years: 1974–1991, Helen Drutt Gallery, Philadelphia, Pennsylvania

Kanazawa Arts and Crafts Competition, invitational exhibition, Kanazawa, Ishibkawa Prefecture, Japan

1990   *Anne Currier and Wayne Higby*, Pewabic Pottery, Detroit, Michigan

Fragile Blossoms, Enduring Earth: The Japanese Influence on American Ceramics, Everson Museum of Art, Syracuse, New York

Archie Bray Foundation, Maveety Gallery, Portland, Oregon

Building a Permanent Collection: A Perspective on the 1980s, American Craft Museum (Museum of Arts and Design), New York, N.Y.

Haystack Faculty '90, Hope Sound Galleries North, Brunswick, Maine

The May Show, Cleveland Museum of Art, Cleveland, Ohio

The West: In Image and Object, Kavesh Gallery, Ketchum, Idaho

1989   *Artful Objects: Recent American Crafts*, Fort Wayne Museum of Art, Fort Wayne, Indiana

Clay & Wine, Napa Valley College, Napa, California

The Eloquent Object: The Evolution of American Art and Craft Media since 1945, Museum of Modern Art, Kyoto, Japan

Exhibit for Annual Spring Forum, James Renwick, Alliance, Washington, D.C.

Helen Drutt Gallery: 15 Years, 1974–1989, Helen Drutt Gallery, Philadelphia; Helen Drutt Gallery, New York, N.Y.

Robert L. Pfannebecker Collection, Kauffman Gallery, Shippensburg University, Shippensburg, Pennsylvania

Surface and Form, National Museum of Ceramic Art, Baltimore, Maryland

Raku: Transforming the Tradition, NCECA, Kansas City Contemporary Arts Center, Missouri

Twenty Years of Contemporary Craft, The Craft Museum of Boston, Boston, Massachusetts

1988 *Contemporary American Ceramics: Vessels*, St. Paul Companies, St. Paul, Minnesota

East-West Contemporary Ceramics, Center for the Korean Culture and Arts Foundation, Seoul, South Korea

A Fine Place to Work: The Legacy of the Archie Bray Foundation, Arkansas Arts Center, Little Rock, Arkansas

Installation: Design, and Architecture, Metropolitian Museum of Art, New York, N.Y.

Master Craftsmen, Nina Freudenheim Gallery, Buffalo, New York

New Gallery Preview Exhibition, Helen Drutt Gallery, New York, N.Y.

Power over the Clay, Detroit Institute of Arts, Detroit, Michigan

Selected Works: 1987–1988, Helen Drutt Gallery, Clark Gallery, Lincoln, Massachusetts.

1987 *American Ceramics Now*, invitational section, Everson Museum of Art, Syracuse, New York, traveling

Ceramic Artists: Works on Paper, The Joe and Emily Lowe Art Gallery, Syracuse, New York

Clay/Fiber/Metal, B. Z. Wagman Gallery, St. Louis, Missouri

The Eloquent Object: The Evolution of American Art and Craft Media since 1945, Philbrook Museum of Art, Tulsa, Oklahoma, traveling

Investigations of the Mind, Helen Drutt Gallery, Philadelphia, Pennsylvania

Symposium Participants Invitation, Napa Valley College Gallery, Napa, California

1986 *American Potters Today*, Victoria and Albert Museum, London, England

Architecture of the Vessel, Rochester Institute of Technology, Rochester, New York

Contemporary Arts: An Expanding View, The Squibb Gallery, Princeton, New Jersey; Monmouth Museum of Art, Livercroft, New Jersey

Contemporary Crafts: A Concept in Flux, Society for Art in Crafts, Pittsburgh, Pennsylvania

Contemporary Raku Ceramics: Tradition Transformed, Odyssey Gallery, San Antonio, Texas

Craft Today: Poetry of the Physical, American Craft Museum (Museum of Arts and Design), New York, N.Y., traveling

The Object as Art: AIDS Benefit, Sotheby's, New York, N.Y.

Raku Tradition, Transformed, Odyssey Gallery, San Antonio, Texas

1985 *American Ceramics: Selected Works*, Swarthmore College, Swarthmore, Pennsylvania

Fired Clay: Vessel and Image, Greenburg Gallery, St. Louis, Missouri

Ceramics, Jane Corkin Gallery, Toronto, Ontario, Canada

International Ceramics, Taipei Fine Arts Museum, Taipei, Taiwan

Surface/Function/Shape: Selections from the Earl Millard Collection, Southern Illinois University, Edwardsville, Illinois

Survey of American Ceramics, Museu de Ceràmica, Barcelona, Spain

13th Chunichi International Exhibition of Ceramic Arts, Nagoya, Japan

1984 *Art for the Table*, Museum Associates, Museum of Contemporary Crafts (Museum of Arts and Design), Windows-on-the-World, New York, N.Y.

Clay: 1984, Traver Sutton Gallery, Seattle, Washington

Clay for Collectors III, The Clay Place, Pittsburgh, Pennsylvania

Clay Vessels: Works by Ten Modern Masters, Palo Alto Cultural Center, Palo Alto, California

Directions in Contemporary Ceramics, Museum of Fine Arts, Boston, Massachusetts

Faculty Art Exhibition, Fosdick-Nelson Gallery, Alfred, New York

Multiplicity in Clay, Metal, Fiber, Skidmore College Art Center, Saratoga Springs, New York

Low Fire—New Frontiers, Greenwich House Pottery, New York, N.Y.

A Passionate Vision: Contemporary Ceramics from the Daniel Jacobs Collection, DeCordova Museum, Lincoln, Massachusetts

Raku and Smoke in North America, American Craft Museum (Museum of Arts and Design), New York, N.Y.

1983 *Soup, Soup, Beautiful Soup*, Campbell Museum, Camden, New Jersey, traveling

American Clay Artists, sponsored by the Clay Studio, Helen Drutt Gallery, Marion Locks Gallery, and Rosenfeld Gallery, Philadelphia, Pennsylvania

Brickworks Artists, Ree Schonlau Gallery, Omaha, Nebraska

Ceramic Echoes, Nelson-Atkins Museum, Kansas City, Missouri

Clay in New Mexico, University of New Mexico, Albuquerque, New Mexico

Contemporary American Ceramics: From Pottery to Painting in Clay, Pittsburgh Center for the Arts, Pittsburgh, Pennsylvania

Art In Western New York, 1983, Albright-Knox Art Gallery, Buffalo, New York

Invitational, American Art Gallery, Atlanta, Georgia

1982   *Ancient Inspirations: Contemporary Interpretations*, Roberson Center, Binghamton, New York, selections traveling

Master Craftsmen, Four Artists, Jacksonville Art Museum, Jacksonville, Florida

East Coast Vessels, invitational, Kutztown State College, Kutztown, Pennsylvania

The Great American Bowl, Art Association of Newport, Newport, Rhode Island

1981   *Beyond Tradition: 25th Anniversary Exhibition*, Museum of Contemporary Crafts (Museum of Arts and Design), New York, N.Y.

Centering on Contemporary Clay: American Ceramics from the Joan Mannheimer Collection, Museum of Art, University of Iowa, Iowa City, Iowa

A Collection of Small Treasures, The Hand and the Spirit, Scottsdale, Arizona

Collector's Choice, St. Louis Museum of Art, St. Louis, Missouri; Detroit Museum of Art, Detroit, Michigan

Crafts '81, Lake Country Craftsmen, Inc., Rochester Museum and Science Center, Rochester, New York

Earthenware USA: New Directions, The Hand and the Spirit, Scottsdale, Arizona

Invitational Exhibition, Archie Bray Foundation, Helena, Montana

Invitational Exhibition: Benefit for ERA, Zambriskie Gallery, New York, N.Y.

Visiting Artists Exhibition, School of Fine Arts, University of New Mexico, Albuquerque, New Mexico

30 Americans, Galveston Arts Center, Galveston, Texas

Art in Craft Media: The Haystack Tradition, Bowdoin College Museum of Art, Brunswick, Maine, traveling

1980   *By Invitation*, Rose Slivka curator, Elaine Benson Gallery, Long Island, New York

Opening Exhibition, Greenwood Gallery, Washington, D.C.

Robert L. Pfannebecker Collection, Moore College of Art, Philadelphia, Pennsylvania

Rochester-Finger Lakes, Memorial Art Gallery, Rochester, New York

Art for Use, Winter Olympics, Museum of Contemporary Crafts (Museum of Arts and Design), Lake Placid, New York

8th Chunichi International Exhibition of Ceramic Arts, Nagoya, Japan

1979   *A Century of Ceramics in the United States: 1878–1978*, Everson Museum of Art, Syracuse, New York, traveling

Contemporary Ceramics: A Response to Wedgwood, Museum of the Philadelphia Civic Center, Philadelphia, Pennsylvania, traveling

Landscape Forms, Helen Drutt Gallery, Philadelphia, Pennsylvania

Language of Clay, Charles Burchfield Center, Buffalo, New York

Raku V Juried Show, Penland School of Crafts, Penland, North Carolina

25th Anniversary Exhibition, Brookfield Craft Center, Brookfield, Connecticut

1978   *Craft Art and Religion*, Vatican Museum, Rome, Italy

Landscape: New Views, Herbert F. Johnson Museum of Art, Ithaca, New York

Raku: The New Tradition, World Crafts Council, Kyoto, Japan

Grant Recipients, National Parks Service, Peters Valley Craft Center, Layton, New Jersey

1977   *American Crafts 1977*, Philadelphia Craft Show, Philadelphia, Pennsylvania

Ceramic Vessel as Metaphor, Evanston Art Center, Evanston, Illinois

Masters Exhibition, Supermud conference, Pennsylvania State University, State College, Pennsylvania

Contemporary Ceramics: The Artist's Viewpoint, Kalamazoo Institute of Arts, Kalamazoo, Michigan

Art Today, Brooks Memorial Art Gallery, Memphis, Tennessee

Viewpoint Ceramics 1977, Grossmont College, El Cajon, California

1976   *American Crafts '76: An Aesthetic View*, Museum of Contemporary Art, Chicago, Illinois

Campbell Soup Tureens: 1976, Cranbrook Academy of Art, Bloomfield, Michigan

Contemporary Ceramics, Hopkins Center Art Galleries, Hanover, New Hampshire

Contemporary Clay: Ten Approaches, Dartmouth College, Hanover, New Hampshire; Wesleyan University, Middletown, Connecticut

Master Craftsmen, Helen Drutt at Marion Locks Gallery, Philadelphia, Pennsylvania

Media Mix: Wayne Higby, John McQueen, and Jessie Shefrin, Fosdick-Nelson Gallery, Alfred University, Alfred, New York

National Raku Invitational, Following Sea, Honolulu, Hawaii

100 Artists Commemorate 200 Years, Fairtree Gallery, New York, N.Y.

6th Biennial Invitational Craft Exhibition, Illinois State University, Normal, Illinois

1974   Inaugural Exhibition, Helen Drutt Gallery, Philadelphia, Pennsylvania

In Praise of Hands, World Craft Council exhibition, Ontario Science Centre, Toronto, Ontario, Canada

Clay Things, East Coast Invitational, Moore College of Art, Philadelphia, Pennsylvania

1972   *International Ceramics*, Victoria and Albert Museum, London, England

1970   *Sherri Smith and Wayne Higby*, Colorado Springs Fine Arts Center, Colorado Springs, Colorado
1969   *Objects: USA*, Smithsonian American Art Museum, Washington, D.C., traveling
           Young Americans 1969, Museum of Contemporary Crafts (Museum of Arts and Design), New York, N.Y., traveling
1965   *Betty Woodman, Maria Martinez, Wayne Higby*, University Gallery, University of Colorado Boulder, Colorado

Selected Public Collections

Arizona State University Art Museum, Tempe, Arizona
Arkansas Arts Center, Little Rock, Arkansas
Brooklyn Museum, New York, N.Y.
Burchfield Penney Art Center, Buffalo, New York
Carnegie Institute, Carnegie Museum of Art, Pittsburgh, Pennsylvania
Craft + Design Collection, Mint Museum, Charlotte, North Carolina
Denver Art Museum, Colorado
Everson Museum of Art, Syracuse, New York
Jingdezhen Museum of Art, China
Joslyn Art Museum, Omaha, Nebraska
LongHouse Reserve, East Hampton, New York
Los Angeles County Museum of Art, California
Memorial Art Gallery, Rochester, New York
Minneapolis Institute of Arts, Minnesota
Montreal Museum of Fine Arts, Canada
Musée Ariana, Geneva, Switzerland
Museum Het Kruithuis, 's-Hertogenbosch, the Netherlands
Museum of Arts and Design, New York, N.Y.
Museum of Fine Arts, Boston, Massachusetts
Newark Museum, Newark, New Jersey
Philadelphia Museum of Art, Pennsylvania
Racine Art Museum, Wisconsin
Schein-Joseph International Museum of Ceramic Art, Alfred University, Alfred, New York
Smithsonian American Art Museum, Smithsonian Institution, Washington, D.C.
The Honolulu Museum of Art, Hawaii
The Metropolitan Museum of Art, New York, N.Y.
The National Museum of Modern Art, Tokyo, Japan
Victoria and Albert Museum, London, England

Commissions

1995   *Intangible Notch*, Arrow International headquarters, Reading, Pennsylvania
2006   *EarthCloud*, Miller Performing Arts Building, Alfred University, Alfred, New York
2008   *Manhattan Canyon*, site-specific installation for Robert McComsey, New York, N.Y.
2009   *SkyWell Falls*, Miller Center for the Arts, Reading, Pennsylvania
2012   *EarthCloud*, Miller Theater, Alfred University, Alfred, New York

Selected Writings and Presentations

2011   "The Story of SkyWell Falls," essay for *SkyWell Falls* monograph. Reading, Pennsylvania: The Foundation for Reading Area Community College.

2010   "Material Matters: Art and Phenomena," curatorial essay for catalogue, 66th Annual Ceramic National. Claremont, California: Scripps College.

"Art and Expectation," opening lecture for 66th Annual Ceramic National, Scripps College, Claremont, California.

"Framing the Future," opening remarks for *Art in the Digital Era*, conference held at South China Normal University, Guangzhou, China.

2008   "kong. flux," opening address, 1st Mathe Coullery Memorial lecture, International Academy of Ceramics General Assembly, Xian, China.

2007   "My EarthCloud," essay for the book *EarthCloud*. Stuttgart, Germany: Arnoldsche Art Publishers.

"EarthCloud Dedication," remarks for the dedication of *EarthCloud*, ceramic installation for the Miller Performing Arts Building, Alfred University, Alfred, New York.

"We Are Here for Each Other," catalogue introduction for the China International Contemporary Ceramic Art Exhibition, Jingdezhen, China.

"Foshan: The Ideal Ingredients," opening statement, 2nd China International Wood Firing conference, Foshan, China.

"Composite: BFA X 4 and the Blue Van," panel introduction, *NCECA Journal* 28, National Council on Education for the Ceramic Arts conference, Louisville, Kentucky.

2006   "On the Obscurity of the Obvious," featured address for *The Studio Potter* magazine, fund raising gala.

"Bridge to Transition," selected quotes, *The Studio Potter* 34/2.

Donna Polseno: Potter's Space and the Earthbound Goddess, exhibition catalogue essay, Eleanor D. Wilson Museum, Hollins University, Roanoke, Virginia, reprinted in *Ceramics: Art and Perception* 66.

2005   "All Roads Lead To Jingdezhen," introduction for *Works by Ceramic Artists from Around the World*, published in conjunction with the 2005 Jingdezhen International Ceramic Art Fair, Jingdezhen, China: Shanghai Fine Arts Publishers.

"Sanbao: East to West, West to East," statement for The Sanbao International Ceramic Art Institute, Jingdezhen, China.

"Beyond Objectness," introduction for Zhang Yushan, ed., *World Contemporary Public Ceramic Art*. Hunan, China: Hunan Fine Arts Publishing House.

"Recalling Bob Turner: Finding the Words," essay for *SOFA: Sculpture Objects and Functional Art. Annual International Exposition*. Chicago, Illinois: Expressions of Culture.

2004   "Shu Yuren: Encounter of Consequence," introduction for Coch, Carla, *Dao·Qi: Spirit and Vessel*. Jiangxi, China: Jiangxi Fine Arts Publishers.

"Zhou Guozhen: The Breath of Life," statement for Zhou Guozhen on the occasion of his Chinese postage stamp.

"Education Is Not a Country," opening address for the Jingdezhen International Ceramic Art Education Conference: Global Perspectives on Ceramic Art and Design, Jingdezhen, China.

"Once More, Into the Unknown," welcoming statement, Jingdezhen International Ceramic Art Education Conference, proceedings catalogue, special issue of China Ceramic Industry.

2003   "Mundane Life: Ceramic Sculptures by Sun Koo Yuh," exhibition statement for Sunkoo Yuh, Western Illinois University Art Gallery, Macomb, Illinois.

"11th Annual Strictly Functional Pottery National", Market House Craft Center, East Petersburg, Pennsylvania.

"A Vortex Of Imagination And Fact," introduction for Bai, Ming, ed., *World Famous Ceramic Artists' Studios*. Shijiangzhuang, China: Hebei Fine Arts Publishing House.

2002   "To Make New Friends Is Glorious: A Commentary on Contemporary Chinese Art," statement for the After Celadon panel, *NCECA Journal* 23, National Council on Education for the Ceramic Arts conference, Kansas City, Missouri.

"Uncharted Territory: Contemporary Chinese Ceramics. A Fourth Generation," lecture commissioned by The Clay Studio, Philadelphia, in response to the exhibition *Chinese Ceramics Today 2002–2004*.

"John Stephenson: Honorary Member NCECA," *NCECA Journal* 23, National Council on Education for the Ceramic Arts conference, Kansas City, Missouri.

"The Qing is Dead, Long Live the Qing," essay for *American Ceramics* 14/1.

2001   "Earth and Fire: The Obscurity of the Obvious," presentation for the symposium *Measure the Immeasurable*, World Ceramic Expo, South Korea: World Ceramic Exposition.

"Jingdezhen: Journal Entries," curator statements for guild.com website exhibition of Jingdezhen Ceramic Art.

"Lu Bing: Making as Intelligence," essay for *Kerameiki Techni, International Ceramic Art Review* 37.

"Ceramic Art: Learning From Each Other," introduction for Bai, Ming, *World Modern Ceramic Art*. Jiangxi, China: Jiangxi Fine Art Publishing House.

"Recognizing Haystack," statement for the 50th anniversary celebration of the Haystack Mountain School of Crafts, Deer Isle, Maine.

"Hot Tea and Magic: The Art of Qin Xilin," *China Ceramic Art* 3, published by China Ceramic Industry.

2000   "Sky, Water, Rocks: A Haystack Workshop," essay for *SOFA: Sculpture Objects Functional Art. Annual International Exposition*. Chicago, Illinois: Expressions of Culture.

"In Recognition of the Space Between," presentation on the occasion of the dedication of the Van Frechette International Friendship Park, Alfred University, Alfred, New York.

"The Spirit of Porcelain," keynote address, Jingdezhen Ceramic Art Conference, *China Ceramic Art* 2, published by China Ceramic Industry.

"Into the Unknown: Imagination and the Space Between," statement for the dedication of new art buildings, Shanghai University, honorary professor presentation.

"A Space Between: The Sculpture of Chen Guanghui," *Kerameiki Techni, International Ceramic Art Review* 34.

"Five Issues," Ceramic National panel, Everson Museum of Art, Syracuse, New York.

1999   "If the Taj Mahal Was Made of Glass," presentation Ceramic Millennium conference, Amsterdam, the Netherlands.

"Contemporary Ceramic Art, Folklore and Fact: The Legend of Alfred," lecture on the history of ceramic art at Alfred University commissioned by The Metropolitan Museum of Art, New York, N.Y.

"Tile Sculpture: Journal Notes," *Kerameiki Techni, International Ceramic Art Review*.

1998   "In the Spirit of a Potlatch," *NCECA Journal* 19, review for the National Council on Education for the Ceramic Arts conference, Fort Worth, Texas, NCECA Honors and Fellows exhibition.

"Sunkoo Yuh: A Man With A Bird Hat," *Ceramic Art and Perception* 33.

"Glaze, Fire, a Poet's Brush: Ceramic Art and Li Jusheng," exhibition catalogue statement, published by Jingdezhen Ceramic Institute, Jingdezhen, China.

"Opening Remarks: China International Summer Program," Alfred China Summer, Jingdezhen, China.

"Closing Remarks: China International Summer Program," for Alfred China Summer, Jingdezhen, China.

Preface for Chinese text: "Survey of Contemporary Ceramic Art: A Global Perspective," published in Jingdezhen, China.

1997   "Sunkoo Yuh: Along the Way", Philadelphia Art Alliance, Philadelphia, Pennsylvania.

"Wayne Higby, Recent Work: An Autobiographical Critique," *Ceramic Art and Perception* 28.

1996   "Imagination," Alfred University commencement remarks, Alfred University, Alfred, New York.

"Philip Rawson," *The Studio Potter* 24/2.

"In Celebration of Ceramics: Philip Rawson's Enduring Gift," *NCECA Journal* 17, National Council on Education for the Ceramic Arts conference, Rochester, New York.

"Walter Ostrom: Don't You Know," catalogue essay for *Walter Ostrom: The Advocacy of Pottery*, Halifax, Nova Scotia, Canada: Art Gallery of Nova Scotia.

1995   "Final Remarks," closing ceremony Jingdezhen Kaolin International Ceramic Art Conference, Jingdezhen, China.

"Li Jiansheng: The Ceramic Work," exhibition statement for Jackson Lee, Nancy Margolis Gallery, New York, N.Y.

"From a Few Seeds a Forest Grows," opening statement for the 1995 Jingdezhen Kaolin International Ceramic Art Conference, Jingdezhen, China.

1994   "Contemporary American Ceramics: An Impression," Fine Arts Lecture Series, SUNY State University of New York, Fredonia, New York.

"Penn State Clay National: Juror's Statement," Penn State University, University Park, Pennsylvania, P.A.

"Touched and Retouched: Ceramic Art and the Importance of the Audience," presentation, Memphis Brooks Museum of Art, Memphis, Tennessee.

1993   "Art: The Importance of the Audience," Ceramic Connoisseurs event, Memphis Museum of Art, Memphis, Tennessee.

1991   "Achievement and the Shoemaker," Alfred-Almond High School, Honor Society talk, Almond, New York.

"A New Spring Wind: The Quest for a Refreshed Vision in Chinese Ceramic Art," report on the 1991 Beijing International Ceramic Art Convention, Beijing, China.

"Expectation: Art, Materials, and the Photograph," monograph, *Craft in the 90s: A Return to Materials*. First Annual Haystack Institute. Deer Isle, Maine: Haystack Mountain School of Crafts.

"Juror's Statement: Anticipation '91," statement for *SOFA: Sculpture Objects and Functional Art. Annual International Exhibition*. Chicago, Illinois: Expressions of Culture.

1990   "Potter's Choice," Wayne Higby, Warren MacKenzie, *Ceramics Monthly* 38/3.

"Making: An Elemental Priority," *NCECA Journal* 11, National Council on Education for the Ceramic Arts conference, Cincinnati, Ohio.

"Art: Bridging the Space Between," Master Teacher Award, University of Hartford, West Hartford, Connecticut.

1989   "The Intellectual and Sensual Pleasures of Utility," *American Craft* 49/1.

"A Search for Form and Place. Wayne Higby: An Autobiography," *Ceramics Monthly* 37/10.

"Landscape into Pots and Vice Versa," catalogue essay for the exhibition of Robert L. Pfannebecker's collection of contemporary crafts, Kauffman Gallery, Shippensburg University.

1988   "Craft Art: Locating Concept and Response," catalogue essay for the exhibition: *10 Advancing the Tradition: An Exhibition of Ten Artistic Viewpoints*. Portland Museum of Art, Maine Craft Society.

"The 'Look' of Craft-Art," opening lecture. *10 Advancing the Tradition: An Exhibition of Ten Artistic Viewpoints.* Portland Museum of Art, Portland, Maine.

"Viewing the Launching Pad: The Arts, Clay, and Education," *The Studio Potter* 6/2.

1987   "Clay in '87," Juror's statement, New Mexico Potter's Association exhibition, University of New Mexico Art Museum, Albuquerque, New Mexico.

"Art: An Illuminating Vocation," University of Michigan School of Art symposium, "Next Steps: Options in the Arts," closing presentation, Ann Arbor, Michigan, November 11, 1987.

"How Many Angles," letters to the editor section, *Ceramics Monthly* 35/2.

"Gifts Born in the USA: The Art of Craft," *The Crafts Report.*

"Giving the Work a Chance: NEA Fellowship Selections in Ceramics 1986," *Ceramics Monthly* 35/2.

"The Answers: Art Education Exhibition Questionnaire," National Council on Education for the Ceramic Arts.

1986   "Something That Can't Be Named," catalogue essay for *Graham Marks: New Work,* with foreword by Dominique Nahas and essay by C. E. Licka, Everson Museum of Art, Syracuse, New York.

"The Vessel: Denying Function," *Ceramics Monthly* 34/10, featured presentation at the Architecture of the Vessel Conference, Rochester Institute of Technology, Rochester, New York.

1985   "Harmonizing Imagination and Logic," catalogue essay for *Useful Pottery,* exhibition curated by Wayne Higby and Graham Marks, Pyramid Art Center, Rochester, New York.

"Drawing as Intelligence," *The Studio Potter* 14/1.

"Gathering Vision," introduction to the special interest group secession, *NCECA Journal* 6, National Council on Education for the Ceramic Arts conference, St. Louis, Missouri.

"The Vessel Is Like a Pot," *American Ceramics* 3/4.

"Craft As Attitude," presentation for *A Colloquium for the Future,* published by the Haystack Mountain School of Crafts, also published by *American Craft* magazine and republished for the exhibition catalogue *Contemporary Arts: An Expanding View,* Squibb Gallery, Monmouth Museum, Princeton, New Jersey, 1986.

"Ted Randall," memorial statement, *The Studio Potter* 14/1.

1984   Artist statement for the Archie Bray Foundation, as requested by David Shaner, Helena, Montana.

"Foreword," introduction for Rawson, Philip, *Ceramics.* Philadelphia: University of Pennsylvania Press.

"Victor Babu: Master Potter," *American Craft* 44/1, cover story.

"New Directions for Crafts People: Beyond the Studio," panel presentation, Empire State Crafts Alliance conference, Corning, New York.

"Innovation: A Matter of Connections," *The Studio Potter* 12/2.

1982   "On Education," opening remarks for the general membership session on education, *NCECA Journal* 7/2, National Council on Education for the Ceramic Arts conference, San Antonio, Texas.

"The Vessel: Overcoming the Tyranny of Modern Art," *NCECA Journal* 3/1, presentation for the National Council on Education for the Ceramic Arts conference, San Jose, California. Republished in *Choosing Craft: The Artists Viewpoint.* Chapel Hill, North Carolina: University of North Carolina Press, 2009.

"Young Americans in Perspective," *American Craft* 42/2.

1980   "Contemporary Crafts in the Art Museum," presentation for the American Association of Museums, Canadian Museums Association joint meeting, Museum of Fine Arts, Boston, Massachusetts.

"One of a Kind Containers and Vessels," presentation, Contemporary Ceramics symposium, Cooper-Hewitt Museum, New York, N.Y.

"Critical Review," *NCECA Journal* 1/1, National Council on Education for the Ceramic Arts, invitational student exhibition.

"Bob Pfannebecker Collection," catalogue essay, Moore College of Art, Philadelphia, Pennsylvania.

"Matter-Memory-Meaning," exhibition catalogue essay, Honolulu Academy of Art, Honolulu, Hawaii.

"The Role of Craftsmen in Contemporary Society," presentation for Panel on the Future of American Craft, Roberson Center for the Arts, Binghamton, New York.

1979   "Aesthetics-Pottery," presentation, National Council on Education for the Ceramic Arts, NCECA-Super Mud conference, Syracuse University, Syracuse, New York.

1978   "Remarks," featured presentation, Super Mud conference Penn State University, University Park, Pennsylvania, P.A.

"The Art in Craft," panel presentation and catalogue statement for the exhibition *Young Americans,* Women's Caucus for Art, New York, N.Y.

1977   "Viewpoint Ceramics," catalogue statement, national invitational, Grossmont College, El Cajon, California.

1976   "Outline for Ceramics," presentation-lecture in conjunction with *American Crafts '76: An Aesthetic View* exhibition, Museum of Contemporary Art, Chicago, Illinois.

1975   "Beaux Arts Designer-Craftsman," juror's talk and statement, Columbus Gallery of Fine Arts, Columbus, Ohio.

Selected Bibliography

Books

Bai, Ming, ed. *World Famous Ceramic Artists' Studios*. With introduction by Wayne Higby, Shijiangzhuang, China: Hebei Fine Arts Publishing House, 2005.

_____. *World Modern Ceramic Art*. Jiangxi, China: Jiangxi Fine Arts Publishing House, 2002.

_____. *Spirit of Modern World Ceramic Art*. Beijing, China: Jianzsu Publishing House, 1999.

Broun, Elizabeth, and William Kloss. *National Museum of American Art*. Washington, D.C.: National Museum of American Art, Smithsonian Institution Press, 1995.

Broun, Elizabeth, and Kenneth R. Trapp. *Skilled Work: American Craft in the Renwick Gallery*. Washington, D.C.: National Museum of American Art, Smithsonian Institution Press, 1998.

Borrman, Gottfried. *Ceramics of the World*. Düsseldorf, Germany: Verlagsanstalt Handwerk, 1984.

Clark, Garth, ed. *Ceramic Art: Commentary and Review, 1882–1977*. New York, N.Y.: E. P. Dutton, 1978.

_____. *American Ceramics: 1876 to the Present*. Revised edition. New York, N.Y.: Abbeville Press, 1990.

Cooper, Emmanuel. *Ten Thousand Years of Pottery*. 4th ed. Philadelphia, Pennsylvania: University of Pennsylvania Press, 2010.

Diamonstein, Barbaralee. *Handmade in America*. New York, N.Y.: Harry N. Abrams, 1983.

Dormer, Peter. *The New Ceramics: Trends and Traditions*. New York, N.Y.: Thames and Hudson, 1986.

Gogarty, Amy, Mireille Perron, and Ruth Chamber, *Utopic Impulses: Contemporary Ceramics Practice*. Vancouver, Canada: Ronsdale Press, 2007.

Hall, Julie. *Tradition and Change: The New American Craftsman*. New York, N.Y.: E. P. Dutton, 1977.

Halper, Vicki, and Diane Douglas, eds. *Choosing Craft: The Artist's Viewpoint*. Chapel Hill, North Carolina: University of North Carolina Press, 2009.

Held, Peter, ed. *Innovation and Change: Ceramics from the Arizona State University Art Museum*. Tempe, Arizona: Arizona State University Art Museum, 2009.

_____, ed. *A Ceramic Continuum: Fifty Years of the Archie Bray Influence*. Helena, Montana and Seattle, Washington: Holter Museum Of Art in association with the University of Washington Press, 2001.

Heyden, William. *September 11, 2001: American Writers Respond*. Easton, Maryland: Etruscan Press, 2002. Cover image.

Higby, Wayne (introduction). *Ceramic Artists around the World*. Shanghai, China: Shanghai Fine Arts Publishers, 2004. Published in celebration of the Millennium Anniversary of Jingdezhen.

_____. *kong.flux*. Alfred, New York: Robert C. Turner Chair endowment fund, Alfred University, 2010.

Jeffri, Joan, and Columbia University. *The Craftsperson Speaks: Artists in Varied Media Discuss Their Crafts*. New York, N.Y.: Greenwood Press, 1992.

Koplos, Janet, and Bruce Metcalf. *Makers: A History of Studio Craft*. Chapel Hill, North Carolina: University of North Carolina Press, 2010.

Lane, Peter. *Contemporary Studio Porcelain*. London, England and Philadelphia, Pennsylvania: A & C Black Limited and the University of Pennsylvania Press, 2003.

Larson, Ronald. *A Potter's Companion: Imagination, Originality, and Craft*. South Paris, Maine: Park Street Press, 1993.

Lauria, Jo, and Steve Fenton. *Craft in America: Two Centuries of Arts and Objects*. New York, N.Y.: Random House, 2007.

Levin, Elaine. *The History of American Ceramics, 1607 to the Present*. New York, N.Y.: Harry N. Abrams, 1988.

Little, Carl, ed. *Discovery: Fifty Years of Craft Experience at Haystack Mountain School of Crafts*. Orono, Maine: University of Maine Press, 2005.

Lovenheim, Barbara, Suzanne Ramljak, and Paul Smith. *Breaking Ground: A Century of Craft Art in Western New York*. Rochester, New York: The Memorial Art Gallery of the University of Rochester, Hudson Hills Press, 2010.

Lu Ping, Chang. *Contemporary Ceramics*. Beijing, China: Central Academy of Fine Arts Press, 2000.

_____. *20th Century Sculpture: Contemporary Sculpture in the West*. Beijing, China: Central Academy of Fine Arts Press, 1999.

Margetts, Martina, ed. *International Craft*. London, England: Thames and Hudson, 1991.

McFadden, David Revere, ed. *Jack Lenor Larson: Creator and Collector*. London, England: Merrel Publishing, 2004.

McInnes, Mary Drach, and Ezra Shales. *Wayne Higby: EarthCloud*. Stuttgart, Germany: Arnoldsche Art Publishers, 2007.

McInnes, Mary Drach, and Wayne Higby. *SkyWell Falls*. Reading, Pennsylvania: The Foundation for Reading Area Community College, 2011.

Paz, Octavia, and James S. Plaut. *In Praise of Hands: Contemporary Crafts of the World*. Greenwich, Connecticut: New York Graphic Society, 1974.

Perry, Barbara, ed. *American Ceramics: The Collection of the Everson Museum of Art*. New York, N.Y.: Rizzoli, 1989.

Peterson, Susan. *The Craft and Art of Clay*. Englewood, New Jersey: Prentice Hall, 2003.

Sewell, Darrel. *Crafting a Legacy: Contemporary American Crafts in the Philadelphia Museum of Art*. Philadelphia, Pennsylvania: Philadelphia Museum of Art, 2002.

Wechsler, Susan. *Low-Fire Ceramics: New Directions in American Clay*. New York, N.Y.: Watson-Guptil, 1981.

Zakin, Richard. *Ceramics: Ways of Creation*. Lola, Wisconsin: Krause Publications, 1999.

Zhang Yushan. *World Contemporary Public Ceramic Art*. Changsha, China: Hunan Fine Arts Publishing House, 2006.

Zhou, Guangzhen. *American Ceramic Artists Today*. Beijing, China: People's Fine Art Publishing House, 1998.

Exhibition Catalogues

Adamson, Jeremy, *KPMG Peat Marwick Collection of American Craft: A Gift to the Renwick Gallery*. Washington, D.C.: Renwick Gallery of the National Museum of American Art, 1994.

Adlin, Jane. *Contemporary Ceramics: Selections from The Metropolitan Museum of Art*. New York, N.Y.: Metropolitan Museum of Art, 1998.

American Studio Ceramics: A Survey of the Collection. Muncie, Indiana: Ball State University Museum of Art, 2008.

Boyle, Richard, and John Heon (essays). *Landscape as Memory 1990–1999*. Helsinki, Finland: Museum of Art and Design, 1999.

Burgard, Timothy Anglin. *The Art of Craft: Contemporary Works from the Saxe Collection*. San Francisco, California: Fine Arts Museum of San Francisco and the M. H. de Young Memorial Museum, 1999.

Clark, Garth, ed. *Ceramic Echoes*. Kansas City, Missouri: The Contemporary Art Society, 1983.

Cochran, Malcolm. *Contemporary Clay: Ten Approaches*. Hanover, New Hampshire: Dartmouth College, 1976.

Danto, Arthur C., and Janet Koplos. *Choices from America: Modern American Ceramics*. 's-Hertogenbosch, the Netherlands: Museum Het Kruithuis Collection, 1999.

Deitz, Ulysses. *Great Pots: Contemporary Ceramics from Function to Fantasy*. Newark, New Jersey: Newark Museum, 2003.

d'Harnoncort, Anne, and Harvey S. Shipley Miller. *Philadelphia Museum of Art: Gifts in Honor of the 125th Anniversary*. Philadelphia, Pennsylvania: Philadelphia Museum of Art, 2002.

Douglas, Mary F. *Allan Chasanoff Ceramic Collection*. Charlotte, North Carolina: Craft + Design Collection, Mint Museum, 2000.

Drutt English, Helen W., and Wayne Higby (essays). *Contemporary Arts: An Expanding View*. Princeton, New Jersey: The Squibb Gallery, 1986.

Drutt English, Helen W. *Contemporary Crafts: A Concept in Flux*. Pittsburgh, Pennsylvania: The Society for Art in Crafts, 1986.

DuBois, Allen. *Working in Other Dimensions: Objects and Drawings I*. Little Rock, Arkansas: Arkansas Art Center, 1994.

Eksŭp'o, Segye Tojagi. *IAC Members' Exhibition: 2004, Icheon World Ceramics Center*. Icheon, Korea: World Ceramics Exposition Foundation, 2004.

Fairbanks, Jonathan L., and Kenworth W. Moffett. *Directions in Contemporary American Ceramics*. Boston, Massachusetts: Museum of Fine Arts, 1984.

Guerin, Charles A. *Colorado Springs Fine Arts Center: A History and Selections from the Permanent Collection*. Colorado Springs, Colorado: Colorado Springs Fine Arts Center, 1986.

Hummel, Charles, and Lloyd Herman (essays). *Craft Art and Religion*. New York, N.Y.: Committee of Religion and Art in America, Inc., 1978.

Kuspit, Donald, and Nancy Weekly (essays). *Alfred Now: Contemporary American Ceramics*. Champaign, Illinois: Krannert Museum of Art and the University of Illinois at Urbana, 1994.

Lauria, Jo. *Color and Fire: Defining Moments in Studio Ceramics 1950–2000*. Los Angeles, California: Rizzoli International Publications, Inc. in association with Los Angeles County Museum of Art, 2000.

Lauria, Jo, Garth Clark, Susan Peterson, Mary Davis MacNaughton, and Ruth Chandler (essays). *Standing Room Only: Scripps 60th Ceramic Annual*. Claremont, California: Williamson Gallery, Scripps College, 2004.

Manhart, Marcia, and Tom Manhart, eds. *The Eloquent Object: The Evolution of American Art and Craft Media since 1945*. Seattle, Washington: Philbrook Museum of Art and University of Washington, 1987.

Master Craftsman. Jacksonville, Florida: Jacksonville Art Museum, 1982.

Monroe, Michael. *Living with Form: The Horn Collection of Contemporary Craft*. Little Rock, Arkansas: Arkansas Art Center, 2000.

Nordness, Lee. *Objects: USA*. New York, N.Y.: Viking Press, 1970.

Perry, Barbara. *Fragile Blossoms, Enduring Earth: The Japanese Influence on American Ceramics*. Syracuse, New York: Everson Museum of Art, 1989.

Piche, Thomas Jr., and Justin Clemens (essays). *Everson Ceramic National: the 30th Ceramic National Exhibition*. Syracuse, New York: Everson Museum of Art, 2000.

Smith, Paul J., and Edward Lucie Smith. *Craft Today: Poetry of the Physical*. New York, N.Y.: American Craft Museum, 1987.

Tarkassis, Kostas. *International Academy of Ceramics: 50th Anniversary Member's Exhibition*. Athens, Greece: Athens School of Fine Arts, 2002.

Tunis, Roslyn, and Margaret Conkey. *Ancient Inspirations: Contemporary Interpretations*. Binghamton, New York: Roberson Center for the Arts and Sciences, 1982, p. 29. Cover.

Turner, Robert (essay). *Wayne Higby*. New York, N.Y.: Helen Drutt Galley, 1990.

Weekly, Nancy. *Wayne Higby: Thresholds*, Buffalo, New York: Burchfield Penny Art Center, Buffalo State College.

Visionaries of the American Craft Movement. New York, N.Y.: American Craft Museum, 1995.

Articles

"1995 American Craft Council Award." *American Craft* 55/6 (October/November 1995).

Aav, Marianne. "Wayne Higby: Ceramic Landscapes." *Kerameiki Techni* 32 (August 1999).

Arnest, Mark. "Vessels of the Land: Retrospective Highlights Ceramic Work." *The Gazette*, April 20, 2001.

Berman, Avis. "Contemporary American Ceramics: Exploring the Sculptural Potential of Pottery." *Architectural Digest* 27/3 (March 1997).

Boughner-Ramsay, Cindy. "Discussion on Education." *NCECA* (Spring 1984), pp. 18–19.

Booth, Sarah. "Renwick's New Treasures." *The Washington Post*, March 14, 1994.

Brel DeJean. "La Porcelain." *Ceramique et du Verre* 101 (July/August 1998).

Carney, Margaret. "The Corsaw Collection of American Ceramics." *Ceramics Monthly* 45/5 (1997), p. 59.

Clutz, Patricia S. "Wayne Higby: A Career that Began in Wonderland." *Philadelphia Museum of Art, 26th Annual Craft Show*, (November 2002). Catalogue feature.

Colborn, Marge. "New Design." *Detroit News*, October 10, 1992.

Ceramics Monthly 21/7 (1973). Cover image.

Dawson, Shirley. "Evolution of an Art: Western New York Artists Still Writing the History of Clay." *Times Union*, November 24, 1993.

Ditmer, Joanne. "Clay Comes Alive at Foothills." *The Denver Post*, May 4, 2001, p. EE.06.

Drutt, Helen W. English. "Poetics of Clay: An International Perspective." *Kerameiki Techni* 39 (December 2001).

_____. "The University of Iowa Museum of Art Ceramics Gallery." *Ceramics Art and Perception* 68 (Spring 2007).

Feng, Shu Dai. "Wayne Higby." *Ceramic Art* 24 (Taiwan) (1999).

Hammel, Lisa. "Out of the Melting Pot: A Vast Diversity of Crafts." The *New York Times*, November 17, 1988.

_____. "Craft Present and Past at 2 Gallery Shows." *The New York Times*, February 2, 1989.

_____. "In Boston, Mystery in Clay and Glass." *The New York Times*, July 14, 1989.

Hartman, Elaine. "City of Jingdezhen: China Adopts Wayne Higby." *Alfred Sun*, 119/27, July 1, 2004.

Haydon, Harold. "Ceramic Bowls Become Landscape Bowls." *Chicago Sun Times*, March 14, 1980.

Higby, Wayne. "An Autobiographical Critique." *Ceramic Art and Perception* 28 (1997).

Jarmusch, Ann. "From *Mesas* through Canyons to the Sea and Back." *American Craft* 41/2 (April/May 1981), pp. 10–13.

Kay, Jane Holtz. "Creative Landscape Containers." *The Christian Science Monitor*, June 26, 1973.

King, Mary. "Mother Vessel." *St. Louis Post-Dispatch*, February 5, 1979.

Klemperer, Louise. "Wayne Higby." *American Ceramics* 3/4 (April 1985), pp. 32–37.

Lees, Nicholas. "Under Fire." *Ceramic Review* 178 (July/August 1999).

Malarcher, Patricia. "Monmouth: An Expanding View." *The New York Times*, March 16, 1986.

_____. "Master Ceramist Injects His Work with Landscapes." *Syracuse Herald-Journal* (2000), p. 20.

Meenan, Monica. "The Coming Collecting Boom: High Crafts." *Town and Country* 131/4970 (October 1977).

Miro, Marsha. "Two Distinct Artists Find Common Ground in Clay." *Detroit Free Press*, March 15, 1990.

Nichols, Sarah. "Contemporary Ceramics and the Vessel Aesthetic." *Carnegie Magazine* 58/1 (January February 1986).

Perreault, John. "Craft Is Art." *Ceramics Monthly* 36/3 (March 1988).

Pfannkuche Bernd. "Wayne Higby: EarthCloud." *New Ceramics* 5 (Germany) (2007).

Pieszak, Devonna. "In Brief." *New Art Examiner* (June 1975).

Rice, Robin. "Focus: Wayne Higby." *American Craft* 57/2 (April/May 1997).

Rushworth, Katherine. "A Smashing Ceramics Show." *Syracuse Herald American*, October 1, 2000.

Seckler, Judy. "Craft in America." *Ceramic Monthly* (April 2007).

Sewell, Darell, Ivy L. Barsky, and Kelly Leigh Mitchell. "Contemporary American Crafts." *Philadelphia Museum of Art Bulletin* 87.371/372 (Autumn 1991), p. 47.

Siegel, Roslyn. "Elemental Bowls: Landscapes in Clay." *The New York Times*, April 5, 1984.

_____. "Show of Ceramics in Varied Methods." *The New York Times*, September 20, 1984.

Silberman, Robert. "21st Century Ceramics in the United States and Canada." *American Craft* 64/2 (April/May 2004).

Sozonski, Edward. "Wayne Higby Porcelain." *Philadelphia Inquirer*, November 29, 1996.

Temin, Christine. "Arch Street: Feast of Crafts." *The Boston Globe*, September 22, 1989.

Ting, Eva. "Jackson Lee: Reinterpreting Tradition." *Ceramics: Art and Perception* 76 (2009), p. 7.

Thorpe, Azalea. "Young Americans 1969," *Craft Horizons* 29/4 (July/August 1969).

Tully, Judd. "Contemporary British and American Ceramics." *Architectural Digest* (October 1990).

Turner, Robert. "Abstract Bowls: Emotional Connections." *Ceramics: Art and Perception* 6 (December 1992).

Voelz, Mary Chandler. "Democracy Rises from the Mud." *Rocky Mountain News* (2002), p. 22.D.

_____. "Interview with Wayne Higby." *Yixing People's Daily*, May 26, 1998.

Wenyibao, Xie Yue. "Emotional Singer of American Views." *National Publication of Chinese Artists and Writers Association*, March 10, 1993.

Film/Video

Objects: USA. Television Française. Producer Adam Saulnier. 1972.

Public television interview. PBS Channels 45/49, Kent State University, Ohio. August 1980.

Interview for *Voice of America*. Jingdezhen, China. September 1985.

Wayne Higby. Public Broadcasting, Channel NJN (Trenton). Producer Anesa Mehdi. October 18, 1987. First broadcast.

CD-ROM, the Permanent Collection, National Museum of American Art and the Smithsonian Institution, Washington, D.C. 1996.

Color and Fire: Defining Moments in Studio Ceramics, 1950–2000. Los Angeles County Museum of Art audiovisual production. Executive Producer Jane Burrell. 2000.

Checklist of the Exhibition

Inlaid Plate, 1967
Stoneware, salt-fired
18¼ × 18¼ × 2 inches
Collection of the artist
p. 22

Inlaid Luster Jar, 1968
Glazed earthenware, raku-fired
13 × 13 × 11 inches
Collection: Ford & University
Galleries, Art Department,
Eastern Michigan University
p. 21

Inlaid Plate, 1968
Glazed earthenware, raku-fired
13½ × 13½ × 3 inches
Collection of the artist
p. 22

Partly Cloudy, 1970
Glazed earthenware, raku-fired
14 × 13½ × 5½ inches
Collection of the artist
p. 31

Blue Channel, 1972
Glazed earthenware, raku-fired
17 × 17 × 2½ inches
Collection: Austin M. Higby
p. 23

Carolina Winter, 1972
Glazed earthenware, raku-fired
15½ × 17 × 2 inches
Private collection
p. 25

Deep Cove, 1972
Glazed earthenware, raku-fired
13 × 13 × 11 inches
Collection: David Owsley Museum
of Art, Ball State University
p. 29

Triangle Springs, 1972
Glazed earthenware, raku-fired
7 × 10 × 10 inches
Collection of the artist
p. 32

Flash Flood Flats, 1975
Glazed earthenware, raku-fired
7¾ × 13¾ × 9½ inches
Collection: John and Andrea Gill
p. 34

Green Terrace Canyon, 1975
Glazed earthenware, raku-fired
13 × 13 × 11 inches
Collection: Marlin and Regina Miller
p. 28

Red Wall Canyon, 1975
Glazed earthenware, raku-fired
17 × 17 × 2½ inches
Collection: Marlin and Regina Miller
p. 24

White Mesa, 1975
Glazed earthenware, raku-fired
13 × 13 × 11 inches
Collection: Sarah H. Morabito
pp. 26–27

Yellow Rock Falls, 1975
Glazed earthenware, raku-fired
14 × 29 × 7½ inches
Collection: Robert Pfannebecker
p. 73

Calico Canyon Overlook, 1976
Glazed earthenware, raku-fired
13 × 15 × 5 inches
Collection: Jack and Helen Bershad
p. 33

Orange Grass Marsh, 1976
Glazed earthenware, raku-fired
9 × 9 × 8½ inches
Private collection
p. 33

Pillow Lake, 1976
Glazed earthenware, raku-fired
10½ × 9 × 8½ inches
Collection: Helen W. Drutt English
p. 33

Tidewater Gap, 1976
Glazed earthenware, raku-fired
15 × 13⅛ × 9⅝ inches
Collection: Arizona State University
Art Museum, museum purchase,
National Endowment for the Arts
Matching Funds Grant
p. 35

Return to White Mesa, 1978
Glazed earthenware, raku-fired
12 × 22 × 13½ inches
Private collection
pp. 54–57

Floating Rocks Beach, 1980
Earthenware, raku-fired
12 × 20 × 16½ inches
Collection: Marlin and Regina Miller
p. 52

Shelter Rocks Bay, 1980
Glazed earthenware, raku-fired
12 × 19½ × 16½ inches
Collection: Robert Pfannebecker
p. 50

Painted Rocks Canyon, 1981
Glazed earthenware, raku-fired
14 × 20½ × 19 inches
Collection: Minneapolis Institute of
the Arts, gift of funds from Peter
and Sandy Butler with matching
funds from the National
Endowment for the Arts
pp. 74–75

Bay Cliffs Mesa, 1984
Glazed earthenware, raku-fired
11 × 19 × 16 inches
Collection: Louis and Sandy Grotta
p. 45

Mammoth Rock Beach, 1984
Glazed earthenware, raku-fired
10½ × 19 × 16 inches
Collection: The Schein-Joseph
International Museum of Ceramic
Art, New York State College of
Ceramics at Alfred University
p. 51

White Terrace Gap, 1984
Glazed earthenware, raku-fired
11½ × 18 × 16½ inches
Private collection
pp. 46–49

Pictorial Lake, 1986
Glazed earthenware, raku-fired
13 × 34 × 9 inches
Collection: Sarah H. Morabito
pp. 69–71

*Study for Black Sky Landscape
Bowl*, 1987
Colored pencil on paper
18 × 23 inches
Collection of the artist
p. 37

*Study for Green Shore Landscape
Bowl*, 1987
Colored pencil on paper
18 × 23 inches
Collection of the artist
p. 12

Chimerical Bay, 1988
Glazed earthenware, raku-fired
11 × 18¼ × 15½ inches
Collection: Barry and Irene Fisher
p. 51

Study for Cathedral Gap, 1988
Graphite pencil on paper
12 × 15 inches
Collection of the artist
p. 72

Study for Emerald Lake, 1988
Graphite pencil on paper
12 × 15 inches
Collection of the artist
p. 72

Temple's Gate Pass, 1988
Glazed earthenware, raku-fired
14½ × 34 × 6 inches
Collection: Smithsonian American
Art Museum, gift of KPMG
Peat Markwick
pp. 76–77

Tower Lands Winter, 1988
Glazed earthenware, raku-fired
15 × 35½ × 8½ inches
Collection: Arizona State University
Art Museum, gift of Roger and
Janet Robinson
pp. 78–79

Haystack, 1990
Ink, brush on paper
8¼ × 9½ inches
Collection of the artist
p. 13

Eventide Beach, 1990
Glazed earthenware, raku-fired
14 × 15¾ × 2¼ inches
Collection of the artist
p. 100

Emerald Tide Beach, 1991
Glazed earthenware, raku-fired
12 × 20 × 15 inches
Collection: Linda Schlenger
p. 85

Midsummer's Bay, 1991
Glazed earthenware, raku-fired
13 × 18½ × 17 inches
Collection: Sarah H. Morabito
p. 87

Night Sands Reach, 1991
Glazed earthenware, raku-fired
11½ × 18¾ × 14¼ inches
Collection: John and Lenel
Srochi Meyerhoff
Smithsonian American Art
Museum, Renwick Gallery only
p. 84

Storm Water Bay, 1991
Glazed earthenware, raku-fired
12½ × 19¾ × 14 inches
Collection: Eugene Mercy
p. 86

Canyon Lake 1, 1994
Black marker on paper
7 × 9 inches
Collection of the artist
p. 114

Canyon Lake 2, 1994
Ink, brush on newsprint
14 × 17 inches
Collection of the artist
p. 114

*Lake Powell Memory—
Cliffs III*, 1995
Glazed porcelain
15 × 17 × 19 inches
Collection: Marlin and Regina Miller
pp. 111, 113

*Lake Powell Memory—
Recollection Falls*, 1996
Glazed porcelain
16½ × 20 × 9 inches
Private collection
p. 117

*Lake Powell Memory—
Stone Pool*, 1998
Glazed porcelain
15 × 18 × 7½ inches
Collection: Helen W. Drutt English
p. 116

*Lake Powell Memory—
Winter Rain*, 1998
Glazed porcelain
16¾ × 22¾ × 9½ inches
Collection: Smithsonian American
Art Museum, museum purchase
made possible by Florence L.
MacIntyre, Henry Sandham, and
Helen Burr Smith
pp. 118–119

Lacuna Rock, 1999
Glazed earthenware, raku-fired
8 × 8 × 5¼ inches
Private collection
p. 99

Silence, 2001
Rubbing, graphite on paper
19 × 23½ inches
Collection of the artist
p. 14

Eidolon Creek, 2002
Glazed earthenware, raku-fired
8 × 11 × 4½ inches
Private collection
p. 103

Green River Gorge, 2002
Glazed earthenware, raku-fired
9 × 9½ × 3½ inches
Private collection
p. 101

EarthCloud computer composite,
2006
Digital print on paper
35 × 46½ inches
Collection of the artist
p. 160

Stone Gate, 2007
Glazed earthenware, raku-fired
14½ × 16 × 6 inches
Collection of the artist
p. 102

Cloud 1, 2011
Pen, ink on paper
30 × 22½ inches
Collection of the artist
p. 159

Cloud 6, 2011
Pen, ink on paper
30 × 22 inches
Collection of the artist
p. 159

EarthCloud Sketch / Gold 1, 2012
Glazed porcelain with gold luster
12½ × 18½ × 4 inches
Collection of the artist
p. 161

EarthCloud Sketch / Gold 3, 2012
Glazed porcelain with gold luster
15¾ × 27 × 7 inches
Collection of the artist
p. 161

EarthCloud Sketch / 4, 2012
Glazed porcelain
15¾ × 27 × 7 inches
Collection of the artist
p. 161

Infinitas, 2012
Glazed earthenware and stoneware
8 feet × 8 feet × 1½ inches
Collection of the artist
p. 141

Intangible Notch sample, 2012
Glazed earthenware, raku-fired
40 × 20 × 1½ inches
Commission for Arrow International
Collection of the artist
(pp. 105–107)

SkyWell Falls sample, 2012
Glazed earthenware and stoneware
10 feet × 4 feet × 1½ inches
Produced in collaboration with
Individuality Art Ceramics, Foshan,
China
Collection of the artist
(pp. 129–139)

Lenders to the Exhibition

Arizona State University Art Museum; Helen and Jack Bershad; David Owsley Museum of Art, Ball State University; Eastern Michigan University Art Gallery; Helen W. Drutt English; Barry and Irene Fisher; John and Andrea Gill; Louis and Sandy Grotta; Austin M. Higby; Wayne Higby; Eugene Mercy; Marlin and Regina Miller; Minneapolis Institute of Arts; Sarah H. Morabito; Robert Pfannebecker; Private collection; Linda Schlenger; Smithsonian American Art Museum; John and Lenel Srochi Meyerhoff; The Joseph-Schein International Museum of Ceramic Art